D1204065

THE ULTIMATE KPOP HANDBOOK

Ordering Information: Quantity sales. Special discounts are available on quantity purchases by corporations, associations, and others. For details, contact the publisher at the email address above.

Printed in the United States of America

ISBN-13: 979-1188195053

K★POP IDOLS WIKI

<2NE1>
<투애니원>

<Meaning: New Evolution of 21st Century>
<Debut: 2009> <Company: YG Entertainment>
<Official Page: yg-2ne1.com> <Offical Weibo: weibo.com/2ne1asia>
<Twitter: twitter.com/GlobalBlackjack>
<Facebook: www.facebook.com/2NE1> <YouTube: www.youtube.com/2NE1>
<Schedule: yg-2ne1.com> <Fan Club Name: Black Jack>

*2NE1 announced official disbandment in 2016

Stage Name: 씨엘 CL
Full Name: 이채린 (Lee Chae Rin) / Faith Lee
Birth Date: 1991.02.26
Birth Place: Seoul, South Korea
Role: Leader, Vocalist, Rapper
Height: 162cm / Weight: 48kg
Bloodtype: A
Zodiac Sign: Pisces
Chinese Zodiac Sign: Sheep
Instagram: chaelincl
Twitter: chaelinCL
Facebook Fan Page: www.facebook.com/
ChaelinCL

Stage Name: Bom
Full Name: 박봄, Park Bom
Birth Date: 1984.03.24
Birth Place: Seoul, South Korea
Role: Lead Vocal
Height: 165cm / Weight: 52kg
Bloodtype: AB
Zodiac Sign: Aries
Chinese Zodiac Sign: Rat
Instagram: newharoobompark
Twitter: haroobomkum
Facebook Fan Page: facebook.com/
parkbom2ne1fansite
*Left Group in 2016

Stage Name: 다라 Dara
Full Name: 박산다라 Park Sandara
Birth Date: 1984.11.12
Birth Place: Busan, South Korea
Role: Vocal
Height: 162cm / Weight: 47kg
Bloodtype: A
Zodiac Sign: Scorpio
Chinese Zodiac Sign:Sheep
Instagram: daraxxi
Twitter: krungy21
Facebook Fan Page: facebook.com/
SandaraParkFanpage

Stage Name: Minzy
Full Name: 공민지, (Gong Min Ji)
Birth Date: 1994.01.18
Birth Place: Gwangju, South Korea
Role: Lead Vocal
Height: 162cm / Weight: 49kg
Bloodtype: O
Zodiac Sign: Capricorn
Chinese Zodiac Sign: Dog
Instagram: _minzy_mz
Twitter: mingkki21
Facebook Fan Page: facebook.com/
ItsGongMinji
*Left Group in 2016

‹2NE1›
‹투애니원›

★WORKS★

2010: To Anyone
2012: Collection (Japanese)
2014: Crush
2014: Crush (Japanese)

★FILMOGRAPHY★

2009: Style (SBS Drama) (cameo)
2009: Girlfriends (Movie) (cameo)
2009: 2NE1TV
2010: 2NE1TV Season 2
2011: 2NE1TV Live: Worldwide (season 3)
2013: Running Man (SBS) EP156
2014: America´s Next Top Model (CBS)
2014: The Bachelor (ABC) - Juan Pablo
2014: The Tim Yap Show (Filipino)
2014: SBS Roommate (Park Bom)
2014: Running Man (SBS) EP195

★TOURS/CONCERTS★

2011: The Party in Philippines
2011: Nolza
2012: New Evolution Global Tour
2014: AON: All or Nothing World Tour

★AWARDS★

2009: Best Asian Newcomer Award (Asia Song Festival), Song of the Month - "Lollipop", "Fire". "I Don't Care", Rookie of the Month, Bonsang, Rookie of the Year (Group), Artist of the Year, Top Seller Artist (Cyworld Digital Music Awards), This Year's Stage, This Year's Song - "I Don't Care", This Year's Album (GQ Awards), Rookie of the Year, Bonsang Award (Top 10) (MelOn Music Awards), Hot New Star (Mnet 20's Choice Awards), Best New Female Artist, Song of the Year - "I Don't Care", Best Female Singer (Style Icon Awards),
2010: Album of the Year - "To Anyone (Dosirak Music Awards)
2010: Bonsang (Top 10) (MelOn Music Awards), Album of the Year - "To Anyone" (MelOn Music Awards), Best Female Group, Artist of the Year, Album of the Year - "To Anyone", Best Music Video - "Can't Nobody" (Mnet Asian Music Awards), Best Female Singer (Style Icon Awards)
2011: Song of the Month - "Lonely" (Cyworld Digital Music Awards), Song of the Month - "Lonely" (Gaon Chart K-Pop Awards), New Artist (Japan Record Awards), Bonsang Award (Top 10), Album of the Year (MelOn Music Awards), Best Vocal Performance Group (Mnet Asian Music Awards), Best New Band In The World (MTV IGGY)
2012: Song of the Month - "I Love You" (Gaon Chart K-Pop Awards), Best Dance & Electronic Song - "I Am the Best" (Korean Music Awards), Prime Minister's Award (Korean Popular Culture & Arts Award), Best New Artist - "I Am the Best" (MTV Video Music Awards Japan)
2013: World Hallyu Star Special Award (Gaon Chart K-Pop Awards), Song of the Summer (MTV IGGY)
2014: Top 10 Album - "Crush" (Bugs Music Awards), Song of the Month - "Come Back Home" (Gaon Chart K-Pop Awards), Digital Bonsang - "Missing You" (Golden Disk Awards), Bonsang Award (Top 10), Best Electronica Song - "Come Back Home" (MelOn Music Awards), Song of the Year - "Gotta Be You" (MTV IGGY)
2015: Favorite K-pop Video Award - "Come Back Home" (MYX Music Awards), Honored Artist - "Come Back Home" (YouTube Music Awards)

★ 2NE1 Fun Facts ★

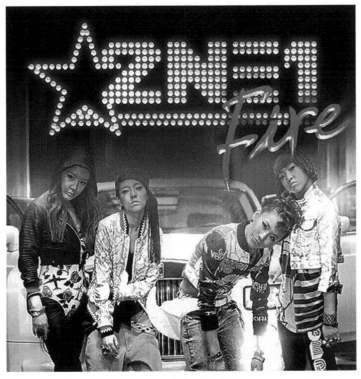

"Fire"
2009.05.06
⟨YG Entertainment⟩

<2PM 투피엠>

<Meaning: "Hottest Time of the Day">
<Debut: 2008> <Company: JYP Entertainment>
<Official Page: 2pm.jype.com>
<V Live: www.vlive.tv/channels/EF7F> <Twitter: twitter.com/follow_2PM>
<Facebook: www.facebook.com/2pm.jype>
<YouTube: www.youtube.com/2pm>
<Fan Club Name: Hottest>

Stage Name: 준케이 Jun. K
Full Name: 김민준 (Kim Min Jun)
Birth Date: 1988.01.15
Birth Place: Daegu, South Korea
Role: Lead Vocalist
Height: 180cm / Weight: 60kg
Bloodtype: A
Zodiac Sign: Capricorn
Chinese Zodiac Sign: Rabbit
Instagram: jun2dakay
Twitter: Jun2daKAY
Facebook Fan Page: www.facebook.com/
JunK-2PM-905681042792399

Stage Name: 닉쿤 Nichkhun
Full Name: Nichkhun Buck Horvejkul
Birth Date: 1988.06.24
Birth Place: California, USA
Role: Vocalist, Visual
Height: 180cm / Weight: 64kg
Bloodtype: O
Zodiac Sign: Cancer
Chinese Zodiac Sign: Dragon
Twitter: Khunnie0624
Facebook Fan Page: www.facebook.com/
NichkhunFanPage

Stage Name: 택연 Taecyeon
Full Name: 옥택연 (Ok Taec Yeon)
Birth Date: 1988.12.27
Birth Place: Busan, South Korea
Role: Main Rapper, Vocalist
Height: 185cm / Weight: 76kg
Bloodtype: AB
Zodiac Sign: Capricorn
Chinese Zodiac Sign: Dragon
Twitter: taeccool
Instagram: otaecyeonk
Facebook Fan Page: www.facebook.com/
OkTaecyeonOf2PM

Stage Name: 우영 Wooyoung
Full Name: 장우영 (Jang Woo Young)
Birth Date: 1989.04.30
Birth Place: Busan, South Korea
Role: Lead Vocalist
Height: 178cm / Weight: 65kg
Bloodtype: B
Zodiac Sign: Taurus
Chinese Zodiac Sign: Snake
Twitter: 0430yes
Facebook Fan Page: www.facebook.com/
JunK-2PM-905681042792399

<2PM 투피엠>

Stage Name: 준호 Junho
Full Name: 이준호 (Lee Jun Ho)
Birth Date: 1990.01.25
Birth Place: Goyang, South Korea
Role: Main Vocalist
Height: 178cm / Weight: 67kg
Bloodtype: A
Zodiac Sign: Aquarius
Chinese Zodiac Sign: Snake
Twitter: dlwnsghek
Instagram: le2jh
Facebook Fan Page: www.facebook.com/
2PM-Lee-Junho-182486515138390

Stage Name: 찬성 Chansung
Full Name: 황찬성 (Hwang Chan Sung)
Birth Date: 1990.02.11
Birth Place: Seoul, South Korea
Role: Vocalist, Rapper, Maknae
Height: 184cm / Weight: 75kg
Bloodtype: B
Zodiac Sign: Aquarius
Chinese Zodiac Sign: Horse
Twitter: 2PMagreement211
Instagram: otaecyeonk
Facebook Fan Page: www.facebook.com/
Chansung2PM

★WORKS★
2009: 01:59PM
2011: Hands Up
2011: Republic of 2PM (Japanese)
2013: Legend of 2PM (Japanese)
2013: Grown
2014: Go Crazy!
2014: Genesis of 2PM (Japanese)
2015: No.5
2015: 2PM of 2PM (Japanese)
2016: Galaxy of 2PM (Japanese)

2016: Gentlemen's Game

★FILMOGRAPHY★
2008: Idol Show (MBC every1)
2009: A Man's Privilege (SBS)
2009: Wild Bunny Ep. 7 (MNET)
2010: Running Man Ep. 4-5, 19, 40, 50-51,
104, 150-152, 162, 195, 201, 234-235, 240,
248, 256, 306 (SBS)
2011: 2PM Show! (SBS)
2011: Hello Counselor Ep. 30, 83, 125, 191,
289 (KBS World)
2012: Beyond the ONEDAY ~Story of 2PM &
2AM~(Documentary Film)
2012-2013: One Point Korean (NHK)
2013: Cool Kiz On the Block Ep. 14-24, 39-
40, 44-50 (KBS2)
2016: I Can See Your Voice S03, Ep. 9
(MNET)

★TOURS/CONCERTS★
2010: Don't Stop Can't Stop
2011: Take Off (Japan)
2011: Republic of 2PM (Japan)
2011-2012: Hands Up Asia Tour
2012: Six Beautiful Days
2012-2013: "What Time Is It?" - Asia Tour

★AWARDS★
2008: Rookie of the Month -"10 Points Out
of 10" (Cyworld Digital Music Charts), Asian
Newcomer's Award (Asia Song Festival)
2009: Disk Bonsang Award, 1st Album:
01:59PM (Golden Disk Awards), Top 10 (Mel-
On Music Awards), HOT Performance Star,
HOT Summer Heat Popularity (Mnet 20's
Choice Awards), Best Male Group, Artist of
the Year (Mnet Asian Music Awards)
2010: Bonsang Award - "Heartbeat" (Cy

world Digital Music Awards), Popularity Award, Bonsang Award (Seoul Music Awards), Top 10 (MelOn Music Awards), Daum's Search Hot Star Award (Special Award, Most Influential Stars (Mnet 20's Choice Awards), Best Male Group, The Shilla Duty Free Asian Wave (Mnet Asian Music Awards), Male Singer Award (Style Icon Award), Most Popular Asian Singer Award (Mandarin Music Honors Awards)
2012: The Best 3 New Artists (Asia), New Artist of the Year (Asia) (Japan Gold Disc Award)

Best Group Video (MTV Video Music Awards Japan), Top New Act (Japan) (RTHK International Pop Poll Awards)
2013: Best Album of The Year (MTV Video Music Awards Japan), Popularity Award (MBC Entertainment Awards)
2014: Best Music Video - "Go Crazy!" (Mnet Asian Music Awards), Global Star Award (SBS Music Festival),
2016: Asian Most Popular Group (2016 KU Music Asian Awards), "Best Album of the Year (Asia) - 2PM of 2PM" (Japan Gold Disc Award)

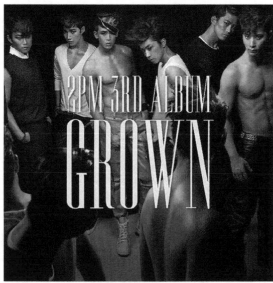

3rd Album "Grown"
2013.05.06
<JYP Entertainment>

TOP 30 Hottest KPOP Idol Bands

<Apink 에이핑크>

<Meaning: A Cube Entertainment (Before Plan A Entertainment)+ Pink (Women) >
<Debut: 2011> <Company: Plan A Entertainment>
<Official Page: www.planaent.co.kr/apink>
<Offical Weibo: weibo.com/ApinkOfficial>
<V Live:www.vlive.tv/channels/FDE29> <Twitter: twitter.com/Apink_2011>
<Facebook: www.facebook.com/Official.Apink2011>
<YouTube: www.youtube.com/acubeent>
<Fan Club Name: Pink Panda>

Stage Name: 초롱 Chorong
Full Name: 박초롱(Park Cho Rong)
Birth Date: 1991.03.03
Birth Place: Chungcheongbuk-do,
South Korea
Role: Leader, Main Rapper, Vocalist
Height: 165cm / Weight: 47kg
Bloodtype: O
Zodiac Sign: Pisces
Chinese Zodiac Sign: Sheep
Twitter: Apinkpcr
Instagram: mulgokizary
Facebook Fan Page: www.facebook.com/
ParkChorong.Apink2011

Stage Name: 보미 Bomi
Full Name: 윤보미(Yoon Bo Mi)
Birth Date: 1993.08.13
Birth Place: Suwon, South Korea
Role: Leader, Lead Vocalist, Main Dancer
Height: 166cm / Weight: 47kg
Bloodtype: O
Zodiac Sign: Leo
Chinese Zodiac Sign: Rooster
Twitter: Apinkbm
Facebook Fan Page: www.facebook.com/
GangsterBomi

Stage Name: 은지 Eunji
Full Name: 정은지 (Jung Eun Ji)
Birth Date: 1993.08.18
Birth Place: Busan, South Korea
Role: Main Vocalist
Height: 163cm / Weight: 47kg
Bloodtype: B
Zodiac Sign: Leo
Chinese Zodiac Sign: Rooster
Twitter: Apinkjej
Instagram: ARTIST_EUNJI
Facebook Fan Page: www.facebook.com/
apink.eunji.fanbase

Stage Name: 나은 Naeun
Full Name: 손나은 (Son Na Eun)
Birth Date: 1994.02.10
Birth Place: Seoul, South Korea
Role: Vocalist, Lead Dancer, Visual
Height: 168cm / Weight: 45kg
Bloodtype: B
Zodiac Sign: Aquarius
Chinese Zodiac Sign: Dog
Twitter: Apinksne
Instagram: marcellasne_
Facebook Fan Page: www.facebook.com/
sonaegi0210

\<Apink 에이핑크\>

Stage Name: 남주 Namjoo
Full Name: 김남주 (Kim Nam Joo)
Birth Date: 1995.04.15
Birth Place: Seoul, South Korea
Role: Lead Vocalist, Rapper
Height: 165cm / Weight: 45kg
Bloodtype: O
Zodiac Sign: Aries
Chinese Zodiac Sign: Pig
Twitter: APINKKNJ
Instagram: sarangdungy
Facebook Fan Page: www.facebook.com/
GangsterNamjoo

Stage Name: 하영 Hayoung
Full Name: 오하영 (Oh Ha Young)
Birth Date: 1996.07.19
Birth Place: Seoul, South Korea
Role: Maknae, Vocalist, Rapper
Height: 170cm / Weight: 49kg
Bloodtype: O
Zodiac Sign: Cancer
Chinese Zodiac Sign: Rat
Twitter: Apinkohy
Instagram: o_h_y_y
Facebook Fan Page: www.facebook.com/
apink.hayoung.fanbase

★WORKS★
2012: Une Année
2015: Pink Memory
2015: Pink Season (Japanese)
2016: Pink Revolution
2016: Pink Doll (2016)

★FILMOGRAPHY★
2011-2012: Apink News (Channel TrendE)
2011-2012: Birth of a Family (KBS 2)
2014: Showtime (MBC Every 1)

Running Man (SBS) - Ep. 162 (Eunji &
Naeun), 177 (Special appearance by Eunji,
Chorong, and Bomi), 202-203 (Bomi &
Naeun), 218 (Bomi)

★TOURS/CONCERTS★
Korea
2015: Pink Paradise 1st Concert
2015: Pink Island 2nd Concert
2016: Pink Party 3rd Concert

Japan
2015: Apink 1st Live Tour 2015 - Pink Season
2016: Apink 2nd Live Tour 2016 - Pink
Summer

Asia Tours
2013: Apink Secret Garden in Singapore -
Vizit Korea
2015: Pink Paradise Asia Tour
2016: Apink Pink Memory Day In Singapore
Mini Concert & Fan Meeting
2016-2017: Pink Aurora Asia Tour

America
2016: Pink Memory: Apink North America
Tour

★AWARDS★
2011: Best New Female Artist (Mnet Asian
Music Awards), New Artist Award (Seoul
Music Awards), Best Newcomer Artist
(Golden Disk Awards), Rookie of the Year
(Gaon Chart K-Pop Awards), Idol Music
Rookie Award (Korean Culture Entertain-
ment Awards)
2012: Hot Trend Award (Gaon Chart K-Pop
Awards), New Star Award (7th Asia Model
Festival Awards)

TOP 30 Hottest KPOP Idol Bands

‹Apink 에이핑크›

2013: Next Generation Global Star (Mnet Asian Music Awards), Bonsang Award - "NoNoNo" (Seoul Music Awards), Digital Bonsang - "NoNoNo" (Golden Disk Awards), Hot Performance of the Year (Gaon Chart K-Pop Awards), Kpop 10 Singer Group (Korean Culture Entertainment Awards), Best Female Dance - "Mr. Chu" (MelOn Music Awards), Best Female Group (MTV Best Of the Best), Bonsang Award - "Mr. Chu" (Seoul Music Awards), Disk Bonsang - "Pink Blossom", Best Female Performance (Golden Disk Awards), Artist of the Year for Female Group (Bugs Music Awards), Song of The Year (December) - "Luv" (Gaon Chart K-Pop Awards), Netizen Awards (Korean Entertainment Art Awards), Best Girl Group (1st Military Chart Award)

2015: TOP 10 Artist (SBS Award Festival), Best Choreography - LUV (3rd European K-POP/J-POP Music Award), Best New 3 Artists (Asia) (29th Japan Gold Disc Award), Kpop 10 Singer Group (Korean Culture Entertainment Awards), Hanbit Awards (Seoul Embassies Day Awards), Disk Bonsang - "Pink Memory" (Golden Disk Awards), Bonsang Award - "Remember" (Seoul Music Awards)

2016: Special Award (KKBOX Music Awards)

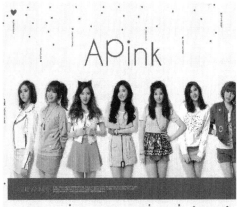

**1st Album
"UNE ANEE"
2012.05.09
‹Plan A Entertainment›**

<AOA 에이오에이>

<Meaning: Ace of Angels>
<Debut: 2012> <Company: FNC Entertainment>
<Official Page: fncent.com/aoa/b/introduce/1303>
<V Live: www.vlive.tv/channels/FEA11> <Twitter: twitter.com/Official_AOA>
<Facebook: www.facebook.com/OfficialAOA>
<YouTube: www.youtube.com/AceofAngels8>
<Schedule: fncent.com/AOA/b/schedule>
<Fan Club Name: Elvis> <Offical Weibo: weibo.com/aceofangels>

Stage Name: 지민 Ji Min
Full Name: 신지민, Shin Ji Min
Birth Date: 1991. 01. 08
Role: Leader, Guitarist, Rapper
Height: 161cm / Weight: 41kg
Bloodtype: AB
Zodiac Sign: Capricorn
Chinese Zodiac Sign: Horse
Instagram: jiminbaby_18

Stage Name: 초아 Choa
Full Name: 박초아, Park Cho Ah
Birth Date: 1990.03.06
Role: Main Vocalist, Guitarist
Height: 160cm / Weight: 42kg
Bloodtype: O
Zodiac Sign: Pisces
Chinese Zodiac Sign: Horse
Instagram: queenchoa_

Stage Name: 유나 Yu Na
Full Name: 서유나 Seo Yu Na
Birth Date: 1992.12.30
Role: Vocalist, Keyboard
Height: 163cm / Weight: 45kg
Bloodtype: O
Zodiac Sign: Capricorn
Chinese Zodiac Sign: Monkey
Instagram: yn_s_1230

Stage Name: 혜정 Hye Jeong
Full Name: 신혜정 Shin Hye Jeong
Birth Date: 1993.08.10
Role: Vocalist
Height: 170cm / Weight: 48kg
Bloodtype: A
Zodiac Sign: Leo
Chinese Zodiac Sign: Rooster
Instagram: dongdong810

Stage Name: 민아 Min A
Full Name: 권민아 Kwon Min A
Birth Date: 1993.09.21
Role: Lead Rapper, Bassist
Height: 160cm / Weight: 43kg
Bloodtype: AB
Zodiac Sign: Virgo
Chinese Zodiac Sign: Rooster
Instagram: kvwowv

Stage Name: 설현 Seolhyun
Full Name: 김설현 Kim Seoul Hyun
Birth Date: 1995.01.03
Role: Vocalist
Height: 167cm / Weight: 47kg
Bloodtype: A
Zodiac Sign: Capricorn
Chinese Zodiac Sign: Dog
Instagram: sh_9513

<AOA 에이오에이>

Stage Name: 찬미 Chanmi
Full Name: 김찬미 Kim Chan Mi
Birth Date: 1996.06.19
Role: Rapper, Maknae
Height: 166cm / Weight: 47kg
Bloodtype: AB
Zodiac Sign: Gemini
Chinese Zodiac Sign: Rat
Instagram: chanmi_96a

★WORKS★
2012: Angel's Story and Wanna Be (debut)
2013: Moya and Red Motion
2014: Miniskirt, Short Hair and Like a Cat
2015: Heart Attack and Ace of Angels
2016: Good Luck, Runway
2017: Angel's Knock

★UNIT BREAKDOWN★
AOA Black (sub-unit): Jimin (guitar), Choa (guitar), Yuna (keyboard), Mina (bass), Youkyung (drums)
AOA White (sub-unit): Hyejeong, Seolhyun, Chanmi
AOA Cream (sub-unit): Yuna, Hyejeong, Chanmi

★FILMOGRAPHY★
2013: tvN "Cheongdam-dong 111"
2015: Naver "Open-up! AOA"
2015: MBCevery1 "AOA - One Fine Day"
2016: OnStyle "Channel AOA"

★TOURS/CONCERTS★
2015: AOA Heart Attack Tour
2015: 1st Concert in Japan: Angels World
2016: Mini Live: Good Luck to Elvis
2016: Summer Concert in Japan: Angels World

★AWARDS★
2014: Best Female Group (SBS MTV), Gaon Weibo Social Star Award
2015: 1st Concert in Japan: Angels World, AOA Heart Attack Tour, Best Promoter Award (SBS Gayo Daejeon), Bonsang -"Miniskirt" (Seoul Music Awards), Digital Bonsang "Miniskirt" (Golden Disk Awards), Hot Performance of the Year (Gaon)
2016: Digital Bonsang "Heart Attack) (Golden Disk Awards), World Rookie (Gaon)

"Short Hair"
2014.06.19
<FNC Entertainment>

\<ASTRO 아스트로\>

\<Meaning: Star\>
\<Debut: 2016\> \<Company: Fantagio Music\>
\<Official Page (Korean): cafe.daum.net/fantagio-boys\>
\<Tumblr (Unofficial, English) with-astro.tumblr.com\>
\<V Live: www.vlive.tv/channels/F6F107\> \<Twitter: twitter.com/offclASTRO\>
\<Facebook: www.facebook.com/offclASTRO\> \<Instagram: officialASTRO\>
\<YouTube: tinyurl.com/ASTROYOUTUBE\>
\<Official Weibo: weibo.com/officialASTRO\>
\<Fan Club Name: Aroha\>

Stage Name: 진진 JinJin
Full Name: 박진우 (Park Jin Woo)
Birth Date: 1996.03.15
Birth Place: Ilsan, South Korea
Role: Leader, Main Rapper, Lead Dancer
Height: 174cm / Weight: 63kg
Bloodtype: A
Zodiac Sign: Pisces
Chinese Zodiac Sign: Rat
Facebook Fan Page: www.facebook.com/
ASTRO-JinJin-1601742860079031

Stage Name: 엠제이 MJ
Full Name: 김명준 (Kim Myung Joon)
Birth Date: 1994.03.05
Birth Place: Suwon, South Korea
Role: Main Vocalist
Height: 175cm / Weight: 58kg
Bloodtype: O
Zodiac Sign: Pisces
Chinese Zodiac Sign: Dog
Facebook Fan Page: www.facebook.com/
astromjofficial

Stage Name: 차은우 Cha Eun Woo
Full Name: 이동민 (Lee Dong Min)
Birth Date: 1997.03.30
Birth Place: Gunpo, South Korea
Role: Vocalist, Visual
Height: 183cm / Weight: 64kg
Bloodtype: B
Zodiac Sign: Aries
Chinese Zodiac Sign: Ox
Facebook Fan Page: www.facebook.com/
chaeunwooofficial

Stage Name: 문빈 Moonbin
Full Name: 문빈 (Moon Bin)
Birth Date: 1998.01.26
Birth Place: Cheongju, South Korea
Role: Main Dancer, Vocalist
Height: 183cm / Weight: 64kg
Bloodtype: B
Zodiac Sign: Aquarius
Chinese Zodiac Sign: Ox
Facebook Fan Page: www.facebook.com/
astromoonbin

<ASTRO 아스트로>

Stage Name: 라키 Rocky
Full Name: 박민혁 (Park Min Hyuk)
Birth Date: 1999.02.25
Birth Place: Jinju, South Korea
Role: Main Dancer, Lead Rapper, Vocalist
Height: 176cm / Weight: 63kg
Bloodtype: O
Zodiac Sign: Pisces
Chinese Zodiac Sign: Rabbit
Facebook Fan Page: www.facebook.com/
ASTRO.Rocky

Stage Name: 산하 Sanha
Full Name: 윤산하 (Yoon San Ha)
Birth Date: 2000.03.21
Birth Place: Seoul, South Korea
Role: Main Vocalist, Maknae
Height: 181cm / Weight: 60kg
Bloodtype: AB
Zodiac Sign: Aries
Chinese Zodiac Sign: Dragon
Facebook Fan Page: www.facebook.com/
AstroSanha

★WORKS★
2016: Spring Up
2016: Summer Vibes
2016: Autumn Story

★FILMOGRAPHY★
2015: To Be Continued (Naver TVCast)
2016: Astro OK! Ready, Astro Project A.SI.A
(MBC Music), The Golden Bell Challenge Ep.
800 (KBS1), After School Club Ep.202, 219,
240 (Arirang TV), Weekly Idol Ep. 256 (MBC
every1), Idol Star Athletics Championships
(MBC), Immortal Song 2 Ep. 282 (KBS)

★TOURS/CONCERTS★
2015: ASTRO 1st Concert "Snowflake"
2016: ASTRO Mini Live "Thanks Aroha"
2016: MBC SHOW CHAMPION in Manila
2016: Kcon LA
2016-2017: 1ST SEASON SHOWCASE (Tokyo,
Jakarta, Bangkok, Shanghai)
2017: The 1st Astro Aroha Festival

★AWARDS★
2016: K-Pop Singer Award (Korean Culture
Entertainment Awards), Male Rookie of
the Year (Philippine K-Pop Awards), Rookie
of the Year (SBS Power FM Cultwo Show
Awards)
2017: Best Japako Discovery (International
K-Music Awards), Hallyu Special Award
(Seoul Music Awards)

"Spring Up"
2016.02.23
<Fantagio Music>

<BTS 방탄소년단>

<Also Known As: Bangtan Boys / Bulletproof Boy Scouts / Bangtan Sonyeondan>
<Debut: 2013> <Company: Big Hit Entertainment>
<Official Page: bts.ibighit.com> <Official Weibo: weibo.com/BTSbighit>
<V Live: www.vlive.tv/channels/FE619>
<Twitter: twitter.com/BTS_twt>
<Facebook: www.facebook.com/bangtan.official>
<YouTube: www.youtube.com/BANGTANTV>
<Fan Club Name: A.R.M.Y (Adorable Representative M.C for Youth)>

Stage Name: Rap Monster
Full Name: 김남준 (Kim Nam Joon)
Birth Date: 1994.09.12
Birth Place:
Role: Main Rapper, Leader
Height: 181cm / Weight: 67kg
Bloodtype: A
Zodiac Sign: Virgo
Chinese Zodiac Sign: Dog
Instagram: bts.bighitofficial

Stage Name: Suga
Full Name: 민윤기 (Min Yoon Gi)
Birth Date: 1993.03.09
Birth Place:
Role: Lead Rapper
Height: 176cm / Weight: 59kg
Bloodtype: O
Zodiac Sign: Pisces
Chinese Zodiac Sign: Rooster
Instagram: bts.bighitofficial

Stage Name: Jin
Full Name: 김석진 (Kim Seok Jin)
Birth Date: 1994.09.12
Birth Place:
Role: Vocalist, Visual
Height: 179cm/ Weight: 63kg
Bloodtype: O

Zodiac Sign: Sagittarius
Chinese Zodiac Sign: Monkey
Instagram: bts.bighitofficial

Stage Name: J-Hope
Full Name: 정호석 (Jung Ho Seok)
Birth Date: 1994.02.18
Birth Place:
Role: Lead Rapper, Main Dancer
Height: 177cm / Weight: 65kg
Bloodtype: A
Zodiac Sign: Aquarius
Chinese Zodiac Sign: Dog
Instagram: bts.bighitofficial

Stage Name: Jimin
Full Name: 박지민 (Park Ji Min)
Birth Date: 1995.10.13
Birth Place:
Role: Lead Vocalist, Lead Dancer
Height: 173cm / Weight: 60kg
Bloodtype: A
Zodiac Sign: Libra
Chinese Zodiac Sign: Pig
Instagram: bts.bighitofficial

Stage Name: V
Full Name: 김태형 (Kim Tae Hyung)
Birth Date: 1995.12.30

Birth Place:
Role: Vocalist
Height: 179cm / Weight: 62kg
Bloodtype: AB
Zodiac Sign: Capricorn
Chinese Zodiac Sign: Pig
Instagram: bts.bighitofficial

Stage Name: Jungkook
Full Name: 전정국 (Jeon Jeong-guk)
Birth Date: 1997.09.01
Birth Place:
Role: Main Vocalist, Lead Dancer, Rapper, Maknae
Height: 178cm / Weight: 66kg
Bloodtype: A
Zodiac Sign: Virgo
Chinese Zodiac Sign: Ox
Instagram:bts.bighitofficial

★WORKS★
2013: 2 Cool 4 School
2014: Dark & Wild
2014: Wake Up (Japanese)
2016: Wings
2016: Youth (Japanese)

★TOURS/CONCERTS★
Korea/Japan/Asia
2014: 2014 BTS Live Trilogy-Episode II: The Red Bullet
2015: BTS Live Trilogy Episode I: BTS Begins
2015: BTS's First Japan Tour-Wake Up: Open Your Eyes
2015: The Most Beautiful Moment in Life On Stage
2016: The Most Beautiful Moment in Life On Stage: Epilogue

World
2015: BTS Live Trilogy Episode II: The Red Bullet
2017: BTS Live Trilogy Episode III: The Wings Tour

★FILMOGRAPHY★
2013: Rookie King: Channel Bangtan (SBS MTV)
2014: American Hustle Life (Mnet)
2014: BTS GO! (Mnet America)

★AWARDS★
2013: New Artist of the Year (MelOn Music Awards), Rookie of the Year (PKCI Awards), Rookie of the Year (Soompi Awards),
2014: New Artist Award (Seoul Music Awards), New Artist of the Year (Male Group) (Gaon Chart K-Pop Awards), New Comer Award (Golden Disk Awards)
2015: Best 3 New Artists Award (Asia) (Japan Gold Disc Awards), Best Choreography - "Dope" (Soompi Awards), Best Korean Act (MTV Europe Music Awards), Best Male Dance - "I Need U" (MelOn Music Awards), Best New Artist (Asia) (Japan Gold Disc Awards), Best Performance Male Group (MBC Music Show Champion Awards), Best World Performer (Mnet Asian Music Awards), Bonsang Award (Seoul Music Awards), World Rookie Award (Gaon Chart K-Pop Awards)
2016: Album Award - "Wings" (Hanteo Award), Album of the Year - "The Most Beautiful Moment in Life: Young Forever" (MelOn Music Awards), Best Album of the Year - "Wings" (UK Charts Awards), Best Artist Award (Male Singer) (Asia Artist

\<BTS 방탄소년단\>

Awards), Best Boy Group (KBS World Radio) 2016: Best Dance Performance - Male Group - "Blood, Sweat & Tears" (Mnet Asian Music Awards), Best Icon Award, Singer (Asia Artist Awards), Best Male Idol (CJ E&M Awards), Best Music Video Boy Group - "Fire" (KBS MV Bank MV Best 5), Best Song - "Fire" (KBS World Radio), Bonsang Award (Seoul Music Awards)

Cultural Minister Award (Korean Popular Taiwanese Annual Chart), Global Artist of the Year (UK Charts Awards), K-Pop Hallyu Star Award (Gaon Chart K-Pop Awards) Culture & Arts Awards), Fandom of the Year - BTS's A.R.M.Y (UK Charts Awards)

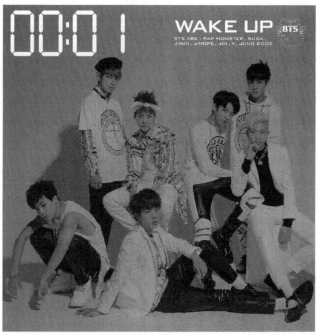

"Wake Up"
2015.02.26
\<Big Hit Entertainment\>

<BIG BANG 빅뱅>

<Debut: 2006> <Company: YG Entertainment>
<Official Page: ygbigbang.com> <Official Weibo: weibo.com/bigbangasia>
<V Live: www.vlive.tv/channels/F13F>
<Twitter: twitter.com/YG_GlobalVIP>
<Facebook: www.facebook.com/bigbang>
<YouTube: www.youtube.com/bigbang>
<Schedule: vip.ygbigbang.com>
<Fan Club Name: V. I. P>

Stage Name: G-Dragon
Full Name: 권지용 (Kwon Ji Yong)
Birth Date: 1988.08.18
Birth Place: Seoul, South Korea
Role: Main Rapper, Vocal, Leader
Height: 177cm / Weight: 58kg
Bloodtype: A
Zodiac Sign: Leo
Chinese Zodiac Sign: Dragon
Facebook Page: www.facebook.com/gdragon
Instagram: xxxibgdrgn
Twitter: ibgdrgn

Stage Name: Taeyang (SOL)
Full Name: 동영배 (Dong Yong Bae)
Birth Date: 1988.05.18
Birth Place: Gyeonggi-do, South Korea
Role: Main Vocalist, Main Dancer
Height: 174cm / Weight: 56kg
Bloodtype: AB
Zodiac Sign: Taurus
Chinese Zodiac Sign: Dragon
Facebook Page: www.facebook.com/taeyang
Instagram: youngbeezzy
Twitter: Realtaeyang

Stage Name: T.O.P
Full Name: 최승현 (Choi Seung Hyun)
Birth Date: 1987.11.04

Birth Place: Seoul, South Korea
Role: Rapper, Vocalist
Height: 181cm / Weight: 65kg
Bloodtype: B
Zodiac Sign: Scorpio
Chinese Zodiac Sign: Rabbit
Instagram: choi_seung_hyun_tttop

Stage Name: Daesung (D-Lite)
Full Name: 강대성 (Kang Dae Sung)
Birth Date: 1989.04.26
Birth Place: Incheon, South Korea
Role: Vocalist
Height: 178cm / Weight: 63kg
Bloodtype: O
Zodiac Sign: Taurus
Chinese Zodiac Sign: Snake
Facebook Page: www.facebook.com/
DLiteKangDaesung
Instagram: xxd_litexx

Stage Name: Seung Ri (V.I)
Full Name: 이승현 (Lee Seung Hyun)
Birth Date: 1990.12.12
Birth Place: Gwangju, South Korea
Role: Vocalist
Height: 177cm / Weight: 60kg
Bloodtype: A
Zodiac Sign: Sagittarius

<BIG BANG 빅뱅>

Chinese Zodiac Sign: Horse
Facebook Page: www.facebook.com/
officialseungri
Instagram: seungriseyo
Twitter: ForvictoRi

_____

★WORKS★
2006: Big Bang Vol. 1 (debut)
2008: Remember
2008: Number 1 (Japanese)
2009: Big Bang (Japanese)
2011: Big Bang 2 (Japanese)
2012: Alive (Japanese)
2016: Made
2016: Made Series (Japanese)

★FILMOGRAPHY★
2006: MTV Korea "BIGBANG: the Beginning"
2011: Mnet, "Big Bang TV"
2016: YG Entertainment, "Big Bang MADE: The Movie"
2016: SBS, "Big Bang MADE: The Documentary"

★ TOURS/CONCERTS ★
2008: Global Warning Tour
2012-2013: Alive Galaxy World Tour
2013-2014: Japan Dome Tour
2014-2015: Japan Dome Tour "X"
2016: Made World Tour
>G-Dragon
2013: One of a Kind World Tour

>Taeyang
2010: Solar Tour
2014-2015: Rise World Tour

>Daesung

2013: D'scover Japan Tour
2014: D'solve Japan Tour

★PUBLICATIONS★
Shouting Out To The World (01.28.2009
ISBN 8992647603)

★AWARDS★
2007: Digital Bonsang (Top 10 Digital Artists) (Golden Disk Awards), Best Male Group & Song of the Year - "Lies" (Mnet Asian Music Awards), Best Asian Newcomer (Asian Music eXtreme Awards)
2008: Dance & Electronic Musician of the Year Netizen Vote (Korean Music Awards), Digital Bonsang (Top 10 Digital Artists) (Golden Disk Awards), Best Male Group - "Haru Haru" (Mnet Asian Music Awards), Hot Trend Musician (Mnet 20's Choice Awards), Artist of the Year & Bonsang, Record of the Year in Digital Release - "Lies" (Seoul Music Awards)
2009: New Artist & Best New Artist (Japan Record Awards), Best Male Artist (Nickelodeon Korea Kids' Choice Awards), Bonsang, Mobile Popularity Award, High One Music Award, Record of the Year - "Remember" (Seoul Music Awards)
2010: Best Song - "Tell Me Goodbye" (Japan Record Awards), Best 5 New Artists (Japan Gol Disc Award), Best New Artist Video - "Gara Gara Go", Best Pop Video - ""Koe wo Kikasete"(MTV Video Music Awards Japan)
2011: Song of the Year (April) - "Tonight" (Gaon Chart K-Pop Awards), Best Music Video - "Love Song" (Mnet Asian Music Awards), Best Worldwide Act, Best Asia Act (MTV Europe Music Awards)
2012: Song of the Year - "Blue", "Fantastic

<BIG BANG 빅뱅>

Baby", Album of the Year (1st Qtr) - "Alive" (Gaon Chart K-Pop Awards), Digital Bonsang (Golden Disk Awards), Best Male Group - "Fantastic Baby", Guardian Angel - "Alive Galaxy Tour", Artist of the Year - "Fantastic Baby" (Mnet Asian Music Awards), Best Fan, (MTV TRL Awards Italy)

2013: Digital Bonsang, MSN International Award (Golden Disk Awards), Bonsang - "Fantastic Baby" (Seoul Music Awards), Best 3 Albums (Asian) - "Alive" (Japan Gold Disc Award)

2014: World's Best Group, World's Best Live Act - "Big Bang Alive Galaxy Tour 2012", World's Best Video - "Fantastic Baby" (World Music Awards)2015: Best Rap & Hip Hop Song - "Bae Bae", Best Pop Song - "Loser" (Korean Music Awards), Song of the Year - "Loser",

"Bang Bang Bang", "I You", "Let's Not Fall in Love", Most Influential Group in Asia (Gaon Chart K-Pop Awards), Artist of the Year, Top 10 Artists, Song of the Year, Netizen Popularity Award - "Bang Bang Bang" (MelOn Music Awards), Artist of the Year (Mnet Asian Music Awards), Most Popular Overseas Group (China's QQ Music Awards), International Song of Summer 2015 - "Bang Bang Bang" (MTV Iggy),

2016: Record of the Year in Digital Release - "Bang Bang Bang", Bonsang (Seoul Music Awards), Special Achievement Award (Special Achievement Award), Song Of The Year By Download (Asia) - "Bang Bang Bang" (Japan God Disc Awards), Best Artist From The World (MTV TRL Awards Italy), Best Selling Foreign Album (China's QQ Music Awards)

Lollipop Pt. 2
2010.02.19
<YG Entertainment>

\<B.A.P 비에이피\>

\<Meaning: Best. Absolute. Perfect\>
\<Debut: 2012\> \<Company: TS Entertainment\>
\<Official Page: www.tsenter.co.kr/03_ts_artist/01_Album.asp?aid=11\>
\<Official Weibo: weibo.com/officialbap\>
\<V Live: www.vlive.tv/channels/FA49D\>
\<Facebook: www.facebook.com/OFFICIALB.A.P\>
\<YouTube: www.youtube.com/TSENT2008\>
\<International Fan Sites: itsbap.com , www.bapyessir.com\>
\<Fan Club Name: Baby\>

Stage Name: 용국 Yongguk
Full Name: 방용국 (Bang Yong Guk)
Birth Date: 1990.03.31
Birth Place: Incheon, South Korea
Role: Main Rapper, Leader
Height: 182cm / Weight: 60kg
Bloodtype: O
Zodiac Sign: Capricorn
Chinese Zodiac Sign: Horse
Twitter: BAP_Bangyongguk
Instagram: bangstergram
Facebook Fan Page: www.facebook.com/
BAP.BangYongGuk

Stage Name: 힘찬 Himchan
Full Name: 김힘찬 (Kim Him Chan)
Birth Date: 1990.04.19
Birth Place: Seoul, South Korea
Role: Sub-Vocal, Rapper, Visual
Height: 180cm / Weight: 69kg
Bloodtype: O
Zodiac Sign: Aries
Chinese Zodiac Sign: Horse
Twitter: BAP_Himchan
Instagram: chanchanieeeeee
Facebook Fan Page: www.facebook.com/
Kim.Himchan.FanClub

Stage Name: 대현 Daehyun
Full Name: 정대현 (Jung Dae Hyun)
Birth Date: 1993.06.28
Birth Place: Busan, South Korea
Role: Lead Vocal
Height: 178cm / Weight: 63kg
Bloodtype: A
Zodiac Sign: Cancer
Chinese Zodiac Sign: Rooster
Twitter: BAP_Daehyun
Instagram: dh_jung_bap
Facebook Fan Page: www.facebook.com/
Daehyun-BAP-356536764424609

Stage Name: 영재 Youngjae
Full Name: 유영재 (Yoo Young Jae)
Birth Date: 1994.01.24
Birth Place: Seoul, South Korea
Role: Lead Vocal
Height: 178cm / Weight: 65kg
Bloodtype: O
Zodiac Sign: Aquarius
Chinese Zodiac Sign: Rooster
Twitter: BAP_Youngjae
Instagram: yjaybaby
Facebook Fan Page: www.facebook.com/
TSent.YoungJae

\<B.A.P 비에이피\>

Stage Name: 종업 Jongup
Full Name: 문종업 (Moon Jong Up)
Birth Date: 1995.02.06
Birth Place: Seoul, South Korea
Role: Main Dancer, Sub-Vocal
Height: 176cm / **Weight:** 66kg
Bloodtype: B
Zodiac Sign: Aquarius
Chinese Zodiac Sign: Pig
Twitter: BAP_Jongup
Instagram: m_jup
Facebook Fan Page: www.facebook.com/
TSent.JongUp

Stage Name: 젤로 Zelo
Full Name: 최준홍 (Choi Jun Hong)
Birth Date: 1996.10.15
Birth Place: Mokpo, South Korea
Role: Lead Rapper, Lead Dancer, Maknae
Height: 187cm / **Weight:** 63kg
Bloodtype: A
Zodiac Sign: Cancer
Chinese Zodiac Sign: Rat
Twitter: zelo96
Instagram: byzelo
Facebook Fan Page: www.facebook.com/
Zelo-BAP-313380485362976

★WORKS★
Single
2012: Warrior , Power, Stop It
2013: Warrior (Japanese), One Shot (Japanese)
2014: No Mercy (Japanese), Excuse Me (Japanese) , B.A.P. Unplugged 2014
2016: Put 'Em Up. Feel So Good (Japanese), Fly High (Japanese)

Full
2014: First Sensibility
2016: Noir

2016: Best.Absolute.Perfect (Japanese)

★FILMOGRAPHY★
2012: Ta-Dah! It's B.A.P (SBS MTV)
2012: B.A.P Diary (SBS MTV)
2012: B.A.P's Killing Camp (Mnet)
2012: Weekly Idol Ep.57 (MBC Every1)
2013: Weekly Idol Ep.85 (MBC Every1)
2013: After School Club Ep.18 (Arirang TV)
2013: Weekly Idol Ep.111 (MBC Every1)
2014: After School Club Ep.45 (Arirang TV)
2014: Weekly Idol Ep.137 (MBC Every1)
2014: You Hee-yeol's Sketchbook (KBS)\
2014: B.A.P Attack! B.A.P Live On Earth 2014 Continent Tour (TSENT2008 YouTube)
2015: After School Club Ep.187 (Arirang TV)
2016: The Boss Is Watching (Feb. 6. 2016) (SBS)
2016: Heart Raiders Idol TV (Apr. 09. 2016) (SBS)
2016: B.A.P's One Fine Day (MBC Music)
2016: After School Club Ep.239 (Arirang TV)
2016: Idol Battle Likes Ep.2 (KBS)

★TOURS/CONCERTS★
2013: B.A.P Live On Earth
2013: B.A.P 1st Japan Tour Warrior Begins
2014: B.A.P Live On Earth 2014 Continent Tour
2016: B.A.P Live On Earth 2016 World Tour

★AWARDS★
2012: Best Male Rookie (Gaon Chart K-Pop Awards)
2012: New Artist Award (Digital) (Golden Disk Awards)
2012: Rookie of the Year (MelOn Music Awards)
2012: Mnet PD's Choice Award (Mnet Asian

<B.A.P 비에이피>

Music Awards)
2012: Best New Artist (Seoul Music Awards)
2012: Super Rookie Idol (Arirang Simply Kpop)
2012: Best New Artist (SBS MTV Best of Best)
2013: World Rookie (Gaon Chart K-Pop Awards)
2013: Bonsang Award - "One Shot" (Seoul Music Awards)
2013: Selling more than 5,000 copies - "One Shot" (Golden Disk Awards Taiwan)
2014: Best Korean Act, Best Japan and

Korea Act (MTV Europe Music Awards)
2014: Best New Artist, Best 3 New Artists (Japan Gold Disc Awards)
2015: Hot Trend Award (Gaon Chart K-Pop Awards)
2016: Best Entertainment Award (Male Group Category) (Asia Artist Awards)
2016: Best Korean Act (MTV Europe Music Awards)

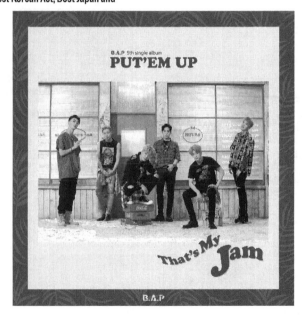

"Put'em Up"
2016.08.08
<TS Entertainment>

<B1A4 비원에이포>

<Meaning: Be the One, All for One>
<Debut: 2011> <Company: WM Entertainment>
<Official Page: b1a4.com> <Official Weibo: weibo.com/chb1a4>
<V Live: www.vlive.tv/channels/FE31F>
<Facebook: www.facebook.com/wm.b1a4>
<YouTube: www.youtube.com/chb1a4>
<Instagram: b1a4ganatanatda>
<Schedule: b1a4.com/2013/schedule.php>
<Fan Club Name: BANA >

Stage Name: 진영 Jinyoung
Full Name: 정진영 (Jung Jin Young)
Birth Date: 1991.11.18
Birth Place: Cheongju, South Korea
Role: Lead Vocalist, Leader
Height: 178cm / Weight: 59kg
Bloodtype: A
Zodiac Sign: Scorpio
Chinese Zodiac Sign: Sheep
Twitter: _jinyoung911118
Instagram: jinyoung0423
Facebook Fan Page: www.facebook.com/
B1A4ArcticFoxYoungie

Stage Name: 신우 CNU
Full Name: 신동우 (Shin Dong Woo)
Birth Date: 1991.06.16
Birth Place: Cheongju, South Korea
Role: Vocalist & Rapper
Height: 182cm / Weight: 64kg
Bloodtype: A
Zodiac Sign: Gemini
Chinese Zodiac Sign: Sheep
Twitter: b1a4_cnu
Instagram: realcnu
Facebook Fan Page: www.facebook.com/
B1A4ChickeNU

Stage Name: 산들 Sandeul
Full Name: 이정환 (Lee Jung Hwan)
Birth Date: 1992.03.20
Birth Place: Busan, South Korea
Role: Main Vocalist
Height: 175cm / Weight: 62kg
Bloodtype: A
Zodiac Sign: Pisces
Chinese Zodiac Sign: Monkey
Twitter: sandeul920320
Instagram: sandoriganatanatda
Facebook Fan Page: www.facebook.com/
B1A4EGGDeul

Stage Name: 바로 Baro
Full Name: 차선우 (Cha Sun Woo)
Birth Date: 1992.09.05
Birth Place: Gwangju, South Korea
Role: Main Rapper
Height: 178cm / Weight: 63kg
Bloodtype: B
Zodiac Sign: Virgo
Chinese Zodiac Sign: Monkey
Twitter: baro920905
Instagram: therealbbro
Facebook Fan Page: www.facebook.com/
B1A4HamBaro

\<B1A4 비원에이포\>

Stage Name: 공찬 Gongchan
Full Name: 공찬식 (Gong Chan Shik)
Birth Date: 1993.08.14
Birth Place: Suncheon, South Korea
Role: Vocalist, Visual, Maknae
Height: 181cm / Weight: 60kg
Bloodtype: A
Zodiac Sign: Leo
Chinese Zodiac Sign: Rooster
Twitter: B1A4_gongchan
Instagram: gongchanida
Facebook Fan Page: www.facebook.com/
B1A4TurChan

_____

★WORKS★
2012: Ignition (2012)
2012: 1 (Japanese)
2014: Who Am I (2014)
2014: 2 (Japanese)
2016: Good Timing (2016)
2016: 3 (Japanese)

★FILMOGRAPHY★
2011: MTV Match Up With Block B (SBS MTV)
2012: MTV Selca Diary Special (SBS MTV)
2012: MTV B1A4 Hot line S1 (Japan) (SBS MTV)
2012: Mnet Wide Entertainment: Sesame
Player S3 (Mnet)
2012: B1A4's Hello Baby Season 6 (KBS Joy)
2012-2013: Weekly Idol Ep.26, 40, 73, 97 (MBC)
2013: MTV B1A4 Hot line S2 (Japan) (SBS MTV)
2014: Go! B1A4 (Mnet America)
2014: B1A4's One Fine Day (MBC)
2014: Weekly Idol Ep.135, 159 (MBC)
2014: Picnic Live (MBC Music)

★TOURS/CONCERTS★
Korea
2012: BABA B1A4

2013: Limited Show [Amazing Store]
2014: THE CLASS
2015: B1A4 ADVENTURE

Japan
2013: BABA B1A4 in Japan
2013: Limited Show [Amazing Store] in
Japan (Zepp Tour)
2014: Listen To The B1A4 (Arena Tour)
2016: The Great World Of B1A4

World
2014: B1A4 Road Trip - Ready?
2015-2016: B1A4 ADVENTURE

★AWARDS★
2011: Hot Debut Star (SBS MTV Best of the
Best)
2011: Best Newcomer (Golden Disk Awards)
2011: Best Newcomer (Seoul Music Awards)
2011: Super Rookies for 2012 (Wave K's
Super Rookies)
2012: Best Male Newcomer (Gaon Chart
K-Pop Awards)
2012: New Asian Artist (Asia Song Festival)
2013: New Artist of the Year, Best 3 New
Artists (Japan Gold Disc Awards)
2013: Disk Bonsang (Golden Disk Awards)
2014: Popularity Award, Bonsang Award
(Seoul Music Awards)
2014: Disk Bonsang Album (Golden Disk
Awards)
2015: Disk Bonsang Album (Golden Disk
Awards)
2015: Bonsang Awards (Seoul Music
Awards)
2016: Best Dressed, Male Singer (31th
Korean Best Dresser SWAN AWARD

\<B1A4 비원에이포\>

"1"
2014.10.27
\<WM Entertainment\>

"Good Timing"
2016.11.28
\<WM Entertainment\>

"Who Am I"
2014.01.13
\<WM Entertainment\>

<BEAST 비스트>

<Meaning: Boys of EAst Standing Tall>
<Debut: 2009> <Company: Cube Entertainment (2009-2016),
Around US Entertainment (2016-Present)>
<Official Page: www.cubeent.co.kr/beast>
<Official Weibo: weibo.com/cubebeast>
<V Live: www.vlive.tv/channels/FE025>
<Facebook: www.facebook.com/beast.unitedcube>
<YouTube: www.youtube.com/beastofficial>
<Fan Club Name: "B2uty" and "B2sties" >

Stage Name: 두준 Doojoon
Full Name: 윤두준 (Yoon Doo Joon)
Birth Date: 1989.07.04
Birth Place: Goyang, South Korea
Role: Leader, Sub-Rapper & Vocalist
Height: 178cm / Weight: 66kg
Bloodtype: A
Zodiac Sign: Cancer
Chinese Zodiac Sign: Snake
Twitter: BeeeestDJ
Instagram: beeeestdjdjdj
Facebook Fan Page: www.facebook.com/
YoonDoojoonFanPage

Stage Name: 준형 Joonhyung
Full Name: 용재순 (Yong Jae Soon)
Birth Date: 1989.12.19
Birth Place: Seoul, South Korea
Role: Main Rapper
Height: 178cm / Weight: 64kg
Bloodtype: O
Zodiac Sign: Sagittarius
Chinese Zodiac Sign: Snake
Twitter: Joker891219
Instagram: bigbadboii
Facebook Fan Page: www.facebook.com/
Jester.Junhyung

Stage Name: 요섭 Yoseob
Full Name: 양요섭 (Yang Yo Seob)
Birth Date: 1990.01.05
Birth Place: Seoul, South Korea
Role: Main Vocalist
Height: 171cm / Weight: 56kg
Bloodtype: B
Zodiac Sign: Capricorn
Chinese Zodiac Sign: Snake
Twitter: all4b2uty
Instagram: yysbeast
Facebook Fan Page: www.facebook.com/
YangYoseob11

Stage Name: 기광 Kikwang
Full Name: 이기광 (Lee Ki Kwang)
Birth Date: 1990.03.30
Birth Place: Naju, South Korea
Role: Lead Vocalist, Visual
Height: 171cm / Weight: 58kg
Bloodtype: A
Zodiac Sign: Aries
Chinese Zodiac Sign: Horse
Twitter: b2stgk
Instagram: gttk0000
Facebook Fan Page: www.facebook.com/
Lee-Kikwang-228339397180242

<BEAST 비스트>

Stage Name: 동운 Dongwoon
Full Name: 손동운 (Son Dong Woon)
Birth Date: 1991.06.06
Birth Place: Busan, South Korea
Role: Vocalist, Rapper, Maknae
Height: 181cm / Weight: 64kg
Bloodtype: A
Zodiac Sign: Gemini
Chinese Zodiac Sign: Sheep
Twitter: beastdw
Instagram: realbeastdw
Facebook Fan Page: www.facebook.com/
KoreanPopUpdate

_____

★WORKS★
2011: Fiction and Fact
2011: So Beast (Japanese)
2013: Hard to Love, How to Love
2016: Highlight
2016: Guess Who? (Japanese)

★FILMOGRAPHY★
2009: MTV B2ST (MTV)
2010: MTV Beast Almighty (MTV)
2010: Idol Maid (MBC every1)
2014: Showtime: Burning the BEAST (MBC every1)

★TOURS/CONCERTS★
2011: Welcome to Beast Airline' (Seoul)
2012: Beautiful Show (Seoul)
2013: Beautiful Show (Seoul)
2014: Beautiful Show (Seoul)
2015: Beautiful Show (Seoul, Hong Kong, Taipei)
2016: Beautiful Show (Seoul)

★AWARDS★
2010: Samsung Yepp Newcomer Award (Golden Disk Awards)
2010: Newcomer Award, Bonsang Award - "Bad Girl & Mystery" (Seoul Music Awards)
2011: Best Male Dance Performance - "Fiction" (Mnet Asian Music Awards)
2011: Top 10 (Bonsang), Artist of the Year (Daesang) (MelOn Music Awards)
2011: Bonsang Award - "Soom & Shock" (Seoul Music Awards)
2012: Disk Bonsang, CeCi K-pop Icon Award, MSN International Award - "Fiction and Fact" (Golden Disk Awards)
2012: Top 10 (Bonsang), Netizen Choice Award, Artist of the Year (Daesang) (MelOn Music Awards)
2012: Bonsang Award - "Fiction & On Rainy Days" (Seoul Music Awards)
2013: Disk Album Award, JTBC Best Artist Award - "Midnight Sun" (Golden Disk Awards)
2013: Top 10 (Bonsang), Best Music Video - "Shadow" (MelOn Music Awards)
2013: Bonsang Award - "Shadow" (Seoul Music Awards)
2014: Popularity Award, Disk Bonsang - "Hard to Love, How to Love" (Golden Disk Awards)
2014: Top 10 (Bonsang), Netizen Popularity Award (MelOn Music Awards)
2014: Bonsang Award - "Good Luck & 12:30), Best Record of the Year - "Time 12:30" (Seoul Music Awards)
2015: Best Male Performance, Popularity Awards - "Good Luck" (Golden Disk Awards)
2016: Disk Bonsang - "Ordinary (EP)" (Golden Disk Awards)

"Fiction and Fact"
2011.05.17
<Cube Entertainment>

<Black Pink 블랙핑크>

<Meaning: "Pretty Isn't Everything")
<Debut: 2016> <Company: YG Entertainment>
<Official Page: blackpinkofficial.com>
<Official Weibo: weibo.com/ygblackpinkofficial>
<V Live: www.vlive.tv/channels/FOO1E5> <Twitter: twitter.com/yg_blackpink>
<Instagram: blackpinkofficial>
<Facebook: /www.facebook.com/BLACKPINKOFFICIAL>
<YouTube: www.youtube.com/c/blackpinkofficial>
<Fan Club Name: BLINK>

Stage Name: 지수 (Jisoo)
Full Name: 김지수 (Kim Ji Soo)
Birth Date: 1995.01.03
Birth Place: Seoul, South Korea
Role: Lead Vocal, Visual
Height: 162cm / Weight: 45kg
Zodiac Sign: Capricorn
Chinese Zodiac Sign: Pig
Facebook Fan Page: www.facebook.com/
BlackPink.Jisoo.kim

_____

Stage Name: 제니 (Jennie)
Full Name: 제니김 (Jennie Kim)
Birth Date: 1996.01.16
Birth Place: South Korea
Role: Main Rapper, Vocalist
Height: 163cm . Weight: 50kg
Zodiac Sign: Capricorn
Chinese Zodiac Sign: Rat
Facebook Fan Page: www.facebook.com/
BlackPink.Jennie

_____

Stage Name: 로제 (ROSÉ)
Full Name: 박채영 (Park Chae Young)
English Name: Roseanne Park
Birth Date: 1997.02.11
Birth Place: New Zealand
Role: Main Vocalist, Lead Dancer
Height: 168cm / Weight: 45kg

Zodiac Sign: Aquarius
Chinese Zodiac Sign: Pig
Facebook Fan Page: www.facebook.com/
BlackPink.Rose.yg

_____

Stage Name: 리사 (Lisa)
Full Name: Lalisa Manoban, Pranpriya
Manoban
Birth Date: 1997.03.27
Birth Place: Bangkok, Thailand
Role: Main Dancer, Lead Rapper, Sub
Vocalist, Maknae
Height: 167cm / Weight: 46kg
Zodiac Sign: Aries
Chinese Zodiac Sign: Ox
Facebook Fan Page: www.facebook.com/
BlackPink.Lisa.yg

_____

★WORKS★
Single Albums
2016: Square One
2016: Square Two

★FILMOGRAPHY★
2016: Inkigayo Ep. 879 (SBS)
2016: M Countdown Ep. 500 (Mnet)
2016: Weekly Idol Ep. 277 (MBC every1)
2016: Running Man Ep. 330 (SBS)
2017: Radio Star Ep. 509 (MBC)

\<Black Pink 블랙핑크\>

★AWARDS★

2016: Best Rookie Award, Female Singer (Asia Artist Awards)

2016: Rookie of the Year, Song of the Year (August) - "Whistle"(Gaon Chart K-Pop Awards)

2016: Best New Artist (MelOn Music Awards)

2016: Weekly Popularity Award (August 22) (MelOn Popularity Award)

2016: Best Of Next Artist Award (Female), Best Music Video - "Whistle" (Mnet Asian Music Awards)

2016: Best K-pop Rookie Group of the Year (KpopStarz Awards)

2016: Best Girl Group, Rookie of the Year (Hallyu K Fans' Choice Awards)

2017: New Artist of the Year (Golden Disk Awards)

"Square One"
2016.08.08
< YG Entertainment>

"Square Two"
2016.11.01
< YG Entertainment>

\<BLOCK B 블락비\>

\<Meaning: Block Buster\>
\<Debut: 2011\> \<Company: KQ Entertainment, Seven Seasons\>
\<Official Page: www.sevenseasons.co.kr\>
\<Official Weibo: weibo.com/blockbofficial\>
\<V Live: www.vlive.tv/channels/FBA71\>
\<Facebook: www.facebook.com/BlockBOfficial\>
\<YouTube: www.youtube.com/7seasons2013\>
\<Instagram: blockb_official_\>
\<Fan Club Name: "BBC (Block B Club)" \>

Stage Name: 지코 Zico
Full Name: 우지호 (Woo Ji Ho)
Birth Date: 1992.09.14
Birth Place: Seoul, South Korea
Role: Leader, Main Rapper & Composer
Height: 182cm / Weight: 65kg
Zodiac Sign: Virgo
Chinese Zodiac Sign: Monkey
Twitter: ZICO92
Instagram: woozico0914
Facebook Fan Page: www.facebook.com/
BlockBZico

Stage Name: 태일 Taeil
Full Name: 이태일 (Lee Tae Il)
Birth Date: 1990.09.24
Birth Place: Seoul, South Korea
Role: Main Vocalist
Height: 167cm / Weight: 57kg
Zodiac Sign: Libra
Chinese Zodiac Sign: Horse
Twitter: BB_taeil
Instagram: 2taeil2
Facebook Fan Page: www.facebook.com/
TaeilTaell

Stage Name: 재효 Jaehyo
Full Name: 안재효 (Ahn Jae Hyo)
Birth Date: 1990.12.23
Birth Place: Busan, South Korea
Role: Lead Vocalist, Visual
Height: 182cm / Weight: 60kg
Zodiac Sign: Capricorn
Chinese Zodiac Sign: Horse
Twitter: blockbhyo
Instagram: bbjhyo
Facebook Fan Page: www.facebook.com/
JaehyoBBC

Stage Name: 비범 B-Bomb
Full Name: 이민혁 (Lee Min Hyuk)
Birth Date: 1990.12.14
Birth Place: Seoul, South Korea
Role: Vocalist and Main Dancer
Height: 178cm / Weight: 60kg
Zodiac Sign: Sagittarius
Chinese Zodiac Sign: Horse
Twitter: BlockB2011
Instagram: bbomb2011
Facebook Fan Page: www.facebook.com/
Lee-Min-Hyuk-Block-Bs-B-
Bomb-183802471687471

\<BLOCK B 블락비\>

Stage Name: 피오 P.O.
Full Name: 표지훈 (Pyo Ji Hoon)
Birth Date: 1993.02.02
Birth Place: Seoul, South Korea
Role: Rapper, Maknae
Height: 181cm / Weight: 64kg
Zodiac Sign: Aquarius
Chinese Zodiac Sign: Rooster
Twitter: pyojihoon
Facebook Fan Page: www.facebook.com/
PyoJiHoon

Stage Name: 경 Kyung
Full Name: 박경 (Park Kyung)
Birth Date: 1992.07.08
Birth Place: Seoul, South Korea
Role: Lead Rapper, Composer
Height: 176cm / Weight: 56kg
Zodiac Sign: Cancer
Chinese Zodiac Sign: Monkey
Twitter: BlockBkyung
Instagram: qkrrud78
Facebook Fan Page: www.facebook.com/
Block-B-Kyung-179144258801167

Stage Name: 유권 U-Kwon
Full Name: 김유권 (Kim Yoo Kwon)
Birth Date: 1992.04.09
Birth Place: Suwon, South Korea
Role: Vocalist, Lead Dancer
Height: 176cm / Weight: 63kg
Zodiac Sign: Aries
Chinese Zodiac Sign: Monkey
Instagram: uk_530
Facebook Fan Page: www.facebook.com/
U-Kwon-Block-B-1414770102106590

★WORKS★

Full Albums
2012: Blockbuster
2016: My Zone (Japanese)

Single Albums
2011: Do You Wanna B?
2014: Jackpot
2015: Very Good (Japanese), H.E.R
(Japanese)
2016: Jackpot (Japanese), Toy (Japanese)

★FILMOGRAPHY★
2013: Weekly Idol Ep. 118 (MBC Every 1)
2014: Show! Music Core (MBC)
2014: 1000 Song Challenge (SBS)
2014: Fashion King Korea Season 2 (SBS)
2015-present: Problematic Men (tvN)
2015: 100 People, 100 Songs Ep. 16 (JTBC)
2015: King of Mask Singer (MBC)
2015: Show Me The Money (Mnet)
2016: Same Bed, Different Dreams (SBS)
2016: Radio Star Ep. 463 (MBC)
2016: Celebrity Bromance (MBig TV)
2016: Saturday Night Live Korea Season 7
Ep. 5 (Mnet)
2016: Weekly Idol Ep. 244 (MBC every 1)
2016: Problematic Men Ep. 58, 59 (tvN)
2016: Infinite Challenge Ep. 472, 474-
475,493 (MBC)
2016: Happy Together Ep. 441 (KBS2)
2016: Celebrity Bromance (MBig TV)
2016: Running Man Ep. 299 (SBS)
2016: Talents for Sale Ep. 7, 8 (KBS)
2016: Radio Star Ep. 491 (MBC)
2016: Radio Star Ep. 496 (MBC)
2016: We Got Married Ep. 347-348 (MBC)
2016: Lipstick Prince (OnStyle)
2016: Laundry Day (OnStyle)

<BLOCK B 블락비>

★TOURS/CONCERTS★
2014: BLOCKBUSTER in SEOUL
2014: BLOCKBUSTER in BUSAN
2014: BLOCKBUSTER REMASTERING
2016: BLOCKBUSTER LIVE

★AWARDS★
2012: New Artist Award (20th Korean Culture Entertainment Awards)
2012: Best Male Video - "Nillili Mambo" (SBS MTV Best of The Best Awards)
2013: Best Male Group (SBS MTV Best of The Best Awards)
2013: Best Fandom (K-Star Best KPop Awards)

2014: Gaon Weibo Social Star Award (Gaon Weibo Chart)
2014: Best Male Dance Artist ("H.E.R") (MelOn Music Awards)
2014: Hot Trend Awards (Gaon Chart Awards)
2016: Best New Asian Artist (Japan Gold Disc Award)
2016: Best Star Award, Singer (Asia Artist Awards)

"Blooming Period" 2016.04.11
<KQ Entertainment>

<BtoB 비투비>

<Meaning: Born To Beat>
<Debut: 2012> <Company: Cube Entertainment>
<Official Page: www.cubeent.co.kr/btob>
<Official Weibo: weibo.com/cubebtob>
<V Live: www.vlive.tv/channels/FD737>
<Facebook: www.facebook.com/btobofficial>
<YouTube: www.youtube.com/officialbtob>
<Instagram: blockb_official_>
<Fan Club Name: "Melody">

Stage Name: 은광 Eunkwang
Full Name: 서은광 (Seo Eun Kwang)
Birth Date: 1990.11.22
Birth Place: Yongin, South Korea
Role: Main Vocalist, Leader
Height: 173cm / Weight: 62kg
Bloodtype: A
Zodiac Sign: Sagittarius
Chinese Zodiac Sign: Horse
Twitter: /BTOB_SEKwang
Instagram: btob_silver_light
Facebook Fan Page: www.facebook.com/
BTOB.EUNKWANG

Stage Name: 민혁 Minhyuk
Full Name: 이민혁 (Lee Min Hyuk)
Birth Date: 1990.11.29
Birth Place: Seoul, South Korea
Role: Vocalist, Rapper, Visual
Height: 173cm / Weight: 61kg
Bloodtype: A
Zodiac Sign: Sagittarius
Chinese Zodiac Sign: Horse
Twitter: btob2mh
Instagram: hutazone
Facebook Fan Page: www.facebook.com/
BTOB.MINHYUK

Stage Name: 창섭 Changsub
Full Name: 이창섭 (Lee Chang Sub)
Birth Date: 1991.02.26
Birth Place: Suwon, South Korea
Role: Vocalist
Height: 177cm / Weight: 64kg
Bloodtype: O
Zodiac Sign: Pisces
Chinese Zodiac Sign: Sheep
Twitter: LeeCS_BTOB
Instagram: lee_cs_btob
Facebook Fan Page: www.facebook.com/
BTOB.CHANGSEOB

Stage Name: 현식 Hyunsik
Full Name: 임현식 (Lim Hyun Sik)
Birth Date: 1992.03.07
Birth Place: Goyang, South Korea
Role: Vocalist, Dancer
Height: 177cm / Weight: 66kg
Bloodtype: A
Zodiac Sign: Pisces
Chinese Zodiac Sign: Monkey
Twitter: BTOB_IMHYUNSIK
Instagram: imhyunsik
Facebook Fan Page: www.facebook.com/
BTOB.HYUNSIK

<BtoB 비투비>

Stage Name: 프니엘 Peniel
Full Name: 신동근 (Shin Dong Geun)
Birth Date: 1993.03.10
Birth Place: Chicago, USA
Role: Vocalist, Dancer
Height: 175cm / Weight: 63kg
Bloodtype: AB
Zodiac Sign: Pisces
Chinese Zodiac Sign: Rooster
Twitter: PenielShin
Instagram: btobpeniel
Facebook Fan Page: www.facebook.com/
BTOB.Peniel.D

————————————

Stage Name: 일훈 Ilhoon
Full Name: 정일훈 (Jung Il Hoon)
Birth Date: 1994.10.04
Birth Place: Seoul, South Korea
Role: Vocalist, Rapper
Height: 176cm / Weight: 64kg
Bloodtype: B
Zodiac Sign: Libra
Chinese Zodiac Sign: Dog
Twitter: BTOB_ILL
Instagram: ilhoonmj
Facebook Fan Page: www.facebook.com/
BTOB.ILHOON

————————————

Stage Name: 성재 Sungjae
Full Name: 육성재 (Yook Sung Jae)
Birth Date: 1995.05.02
Birth Place: Suwon, South Korea
Role: Vocalist, Rapper, Maknae
Height: 180cm / Weight:68kg
Bloodtype: A
Zodiac Sign: Taurus
Chinese Zodiac Sign: Pig
Twitter: BTOB_6SJ
Instagram: 6_zalddow
Facebook Fan Page: www.facebook.com/

BTOB.SUNGJAE

————————————

★SUB UNIT★
2016: BtoB Blue - Eunkwang, Changsub, Hyunsik and Sungjae

★WORKS★
Full Albums
2015: Complete
2016: 24/7

Single Albums
2012: "Insane", "Father", "Irresistible Lips", "WOW", "I Only Know Love"
2013: "2nd Confession", "When I Was Your Man", "Thriller"
2014: "Beep Beep", "You're So Fly", "You Can Cry", "The Winter's Tale"
2014: WOW (Japanese)
2015: "It's Okay", "Way Back Home"
2015: "Mirai (Ashita)", "Natsuiro MY GIRL" (Japanese)
2016: "Remeber That", "I Want to Vacation", "Pray (I'll Be Your Man)"
2016: "Dear Bride", "L.U.V", "Christmas Time" (Japanese)

★FILMOGRAPHY★
2012: Amazon (Mnet)
2012: I Live in Cheongdam-dong (JTBC)
2012: MTV Diary (SBS MTV)
2012: Gurupop Show Ep. 11 (MBC every1)
2012-2016: Weekly Idol Ep. 43, 66, 98, 113, 136, 156, 179, 206, 260,261
2013-2016: After School Club Ep. 23, 47,65, 109, 206 (Arirang)
2013-2016: Idol Star Athletic Championships (MBC)
2013: The Heirs Ep. 4 (SBS)

\<BtoB 비투비\>

2013: We Got Married Global Edition Ep. 7-8 (MBC)
2013: A Song For You S2 Ep.6 (KBS World)
2013: Monstar Ep. 1,2,6,9 (Mnet)
2013: SNL Korea 4 Ep. 30 (tvN)
2013: When a Man Falls in Love Ep. 8 (MBC)
2013: B+ Diary (SBS MTV)
2014: A Song For You S3 Ep. 1, 7 (KBS World)
2014: Beatles Code 3D (Mnet)
2014: Cool Men (SBS MTV)
2015: Star King Ep. 399 (SBS)
2015: We Got Married (MBC)
2015: The Village: Achiara's Secret Ep. 14 (SBS)
2016: The Boss is Watching (SBS)
2016: Enter-K (YTN)
2016: Let's Go! Dream Team S2 Ep. 335-336 (KBS)
2016: Battle Trip (KBS)

★TOURS/CONCERTS★
2013: United Cube Concert
2014: 1st Concert: Hello Melody in Seoul
2015: I'll Be Your Melody
2015: 1st Concert: Hello Melody in Busan
2015: The Secret Diary (Japan Tour)
2015: 2nd Concert: Born to Beat Time
2016: BTOB Zepp Tour 2016 B-Loved
2016: Born to Beat Time: Encore Concert

★AWARDS★
2012: Rookie of the Month - "WOW" (Cyworld Digital Music Awards)
2013: Next Generation Star (Golden Disk Awards)
2015: Singer of the Year (KBS Music Festival)
2016: Best Vocal Group (Golden Disk Awards)
2016: Ballad Award (Seoul Music Awards)
2016: 1st Place (KBS Immortal Song 2)

"Complete"
2015.06.29
\<Cube Entertainment\>

"24/7"
2016.12.07
\<Cube Entertainment\>

<C.N. BLUE 씨앤블루>

<Meaning: CN (Code Name) BLUE (Burning, Lovely, Untouchable, Emotional)
<Debut: 2010> <Company: FNC Entertainment>
<Official Page: fncent.com/CNBLUE> <Official Weibo: weibo.com/cnblue>
<V Live: www.vlive.tv/channels/EBFF>
<Twitter: twitter.com/CNBLUE_4>
<Facebook: /www.facebook.com/CNBLUEOfficial>
<YouTube: www.youtube.com/CNBLUE>
<Schedule: fncent.com/CNBLUE/b/schedule>
<Fan Club Name: Boice>

Stage Name: 용화 YongHwa
Full Name: 정용화 (Jung Yong Hwa)
Birth Date: 1989.06.22
Birth Place:
Role: Lead Vocal, Guitar, Leader
Height: 180cm
Weight: 63kg
Bloodtype: A
Zodiac Sign: Cancer
Chinese Zodiac Sign: Snake
Facebook Fan Page: www.facebook.com/
JUNG-YONG-HWA-129849583701234
Instagram: jyheffect0622
Twitter: jyheffect

Stage Name: 종현 JongHyun
Full Name: 이종현 (Lee Jong Hyun)
Birth Date: 1990.05.15
Birth Place:
Role: Lead Vocal, Guitar
Height: 182cm
Weight: 72kg
Bloodtype: O
Zodiac Sign: Taurus
Chinese Zodiac Sign: Horse
Facebook Fan Page: www.facebook.com/
LeeJonghyun/
Instagram: cnbluegt
Twitter: cnbluegt

Stage Name: 민혁 MinHyuk
Full Name: 강민혁 (Kang Min Hyuk)
Birth Date: 1991.06.28
Birth Place:
Role: Drum
Height: 184cm
Weight: 67kg
Bloodtype: A
Zodiac Sign: Cancer
Chinese Zodiac Sign: Sheep
Facebook Fan Page: www.facebook.com/
OFFICIAL.MINHYUK.CNB/
Instagram: mr_kanggun
Twitter: MR_KANGGUN

Stage Name: 정신 JungShin
Full Name: 이정신 (Lee Jung Shin)
Birth Date: 1991.09.15
Birth Place:
Role: Bass, Rap, Maknae
Height: 188cm
Weight: 72kg
Bloodtype: A
Zodiac Sign: Virgo
Chinese Zodiac Sign: Sheep
Facebook Fan Page: www.facebook.com/
OFFICIAL.MINHYUK.CNB/
Instagram: mr_kanggun
Twitter: MR_KANGGUN

\<C.N. BLUE 씨앤블루\>

★WORKS★

2010: Thank U (Japanese)
2011: First Step (Korean)
2011: 392 (Japanese)
2012: Code Name Blue (Japanese)
2013: What Turns You On? (Japanese)
2014: Wave (Japanese)
2015: 2gether (Korean)
2015: Colors (Japanese)
2016: Euphoria (Japanese)

★TOURS/CONCERTS★

Korea/Japan/Asia
2011-2012: Blue Storm Asia Tour
2013: Blue Moon World Tour
2014: Can't Stop Tour
2015-2016: Live "Come Together"

★AWARDS★

2010: Digital Music Bonsang - "I'm a Loner", "Love" (Golden Disk Awards)
2010: Rookie Award (Seoul Music Awards)
2010: Best Male Rookie (Mnet Asian Music Awards)
2010: Best Newcomer Award, Top 10 (MelOn Music Awards)
2010: Rookie of the Month, Rookie of the Year - "I'm a Loner" (Cyworld Digital Music Awards)
2010: Streaming Award (Gaon Chart Grand Opening Awards)
2010: Rookie of the Year (Bugs Music Awards)
2010: New Style Icon, Singer (Style Icon Awards)
2011: Best Band Performance (Mnet Asian Music Awards)
2011: Music Style - Best Rock - "Intuition" (MelOn Music Awards)
2011: Song of the Month - "Intuition" (Cyworld Digital Music Awards)
2011: Rock Song of the Year - "Intuition" (Bugs Music Awards)
2011: 2nd Prize, Cultural Minister of Finance Award (Korean Popular Culture and Arts Awards)
2011: 1st Prize, Rock Award (KOMCA Music Awards)
2011: Favorite Asian Artist (You2Play Awards (Thailand))
2012: Vivi Dream Award, Best Asian Group Award (Golden Disk Awards)
2013: Hallyu Special Award (Gaon Chart K-Pop Awards)
2013: 3rd Prize, International Sharing Award (Sharing Happiness Awards)
2014: Digital Music Bonsang - "I'm Sorry", Goodwill Star Award (Golden Disk Awards)
2014: Best Band Performance - "Can't Stop" (Mnet Asian Music Awards)
2014: Music Style - Best Rock - "Can't Stop" (MelOn Music Awards)
2014: 2nd Prize, Best Band Award (YinYue-Tai V-Chart Awards)
2014: 1st Prize, Gaon Weibo Chart Awards (Gaon Weibo Chart Awards)
2014: Selling more than 5.000 copies - "Blue Hits for Asia (CNBLUE's special album)" (Golden Disk in Taiwan)
2014: 1st Prize, Asia Best Group (2015 iQIYI Night Awards)
2014: Syrup Best Band Award (SBS Gayo Daejeon)
2014: Best Band Award (SBS MTV Best of the Best)
2015: Disk Bonsang - "Can't Stop", China Goodwill Star Award, iQIYI Popularity Award, Ceci Asia Icon Award (Golden Disk Awards)
2015: Best Band Performance - "Cinderella" (Mnet Asian Music Awards)

<C.N. BLUE 씨앤블루>

2015: 15th Prize, Foreign Popular Group Award (Top Chinese Music Awards)
2016: Disk Bonsang - "2gether" (Golden Disk Awards)
2016: Best Band Performance - "You're So Fine" (Mnet Asian Music Awards)

"Re: BLUE"
2013.01.14
<FNC Entertainment>

<EXID 이엑스아이디>

<Meaning: Exceed In Dreaming>
<Debut: 2012> <Company: Banana Culture Entertainment>
<Official Page: cafe.daum.net/exid>
<International Fan Site: exidworldintl.com>
<Official Weibo: weibo.com/EXIDofficial>
<V Live: www.vlive.tv/channels/F9BAF>
<Facebook: www.facebook.com/EXIDofficial>
<YouTube: www.youtube.com/OfficialEXID> <Instagram: exidofficial>
<Fan Club Name: "L.E.G.O/L.E.G.G.O">

Stage Name: 솔지 Solji
Full Name: 허솔지 (Heo Sol Ji)
Birth Date: 1989.01.10
Birth Place: Seongnam, South Korea
Role: Leader, Main Vocalist
Height: 170cm/51kg
Bloodtype: O
Zodiac Sign: Capricorn
Chinese Zodiac Sign: Dragon
Instagram: soul.g_heo
Facebook Fan Page: www.facebook.com/
Solji-EXID-276684109113958

Stage Name: 엘리 LE
Full Name: 안효진 (Ahn Hyo Jin)
Birth Date: 1991.12.10
Birth Place: Cheonan, South Korea
Role: Main Rapper, Lead Dancer
Height: 168cm / Weight: 50kg
Bloodtype: AB
Zodiac Sign: Sagittarius
Chinese Zodiac Sign: Sheep
Instagram: x_xellybabyx
Facebook Fan Page: www.facebook.com/
EXID.AhnHyoJin

Stage Name: 하니 Hani
Full Name: 안희연 (Ahn Hee Yeon)
Birth Date: 1992.05.01
Birth Place: Seoul, South Korea
Role: Lead Vocalist, Visual
Height: 168cm / Weight: 50kg
Bloodtype: AB
Zodiac Sign: Taurus
Chinese Zodiac Sign: Monkey
Instagram: ahnhani_92
Facebook Fan Page: www.facebook.com/
EXID.HaniAhn

Stage Name: 혜린 Hyerin
Full Name: 서혜린 (Seo Hye Rin)
Birth Date: 1993.08.23
Birth Place: Gwangju, South Korea
Role: Lead Vocalist
Height: 165cm / Weight: 47kg
Bloodtype: O
Zodiac Sign: Virgo
Chinese Zodiac Sign: Rooster
Instagram: hyeliniseo
Facebook Fan Page: www.facebook.com/
Hyerin-EXID-276590255783466

<EXID 이엑스아이디>

Stage Name: 정화 Junghwa
Full Name: 박정화 (Park Jung Hwa)
Birth Date: 1995.05.08
Birth Place: Anyang, South Korea
Role: Main Dancer, Vocalist, Rapper, Maknae
Height: 169cm / Weight: 48kg
Bloodtype: A
Zodiac Sign: Taurus
Chinese Zodiac Sign: Pig
Instagram: junghwa_0508
Facebook Fan Page: www.facebook.com/
EXID-Junghwa-정화-433641836805298

★SUB UNITS★
Dasoni (2013)/SoljiHani (2016) - Hani, Solji

★WORKS★
Full Albums
2016: Street

Single Albums
2012: Whoz That Girl, I Feel Good, Every Night
2014: Up & Down
2015: Ah Yeah, Hot Pink
2016: L.I.E

Dasoni (2013) SoljiHani (2016)
2013: Good Bye, Said So Often
2016: Only One

★FILMOGRAPHY★
2014: Idol School Ep. 11 (MBC Music)
2014: Weekly Idol Ep. 178 (MBC Every1)
2015: Immortal Song 2 Ep. 182 (KBS)
2015: Hello Counselor Ep. 207 (KBS)
2015: Weekly Idol Ep. 197 (MBC Every1)
2015: Yaman TV (Mnet)
2015: Idol Athletics Championship Bronze
Medal (Archery - W) (MBC)
2015: Weekly Idol Ep. 226 (MBC Every1)
2015: Running Man Ep. 237 (SBS)
2015: Gourmet Road Ep. 233 (K-STAR)
2015: EXID Showtime (MBC Every1)
2015: Idol Athletics Championship Gold
Medal (400m Relay Race - W) (MBC)
2015: Running Man Ep. 275 (SBS)
2015: Hello Counselor Ep. 250 (KBS)
2016: Bon Boon Olympic (KBS)
2016: A Look At Myself Ep. 23 (KBS)
2016: Idol Athletics Championship Gold
Medal (Wrestling - W) Gold Medal (Archery
- W) Silver Medal (400m Relay Race - W)
(MBC)
2016: Weekly Idol Ep. 245 - 270, 275 (MBC
Every1)
2016: Idol & Family National Singing
Competition (KBS)
2016: Happy Together Ep. 461 (KBS2)
2016: Battle Trip Ep. 2-3 (KBS)
2016: Weekly Idol Ep. 254 (MBC Every1)

★TOURS/CONCERTS★
2016: EXID's LEGGO SHOW
2016: 1st EXID LEGGO PARTY

★AWARDS★
2012: Super Rookie Idol of the Year
(Arirang's Simply K-Pop Awards)
2012: Rookie Award (Korean Culture and
Entertainment Awards)
2015: Discovery of the Year - 2014 (Gaon
Chart K-Pop Awards)
2015: Bonsang (Seoul Music Awards)
2015: MBC Music Star Award (MelOn Music
Awards)
2015: Best Champion Songs of 2015 - "Ah
Yeah", Best Performance - Female - "Hot
Pink" (MBC Music Show Champion

Awards)
2015: Star Awards (Cable TV Broadast Awards)
2016: Digital Bonsang (Golden Disk Awards)
2016: Bonsang (Seoul Music Awards)
2016: Artist of the Year (Korea Assembly Grand Award)
2016: Best Breakout Artist (YinYueTai V Chart Awards)
2016: Platinum Disc Certification in Digital Sales (Sony Music Sales Awards)

"Ah Yeah"
2015.04.13
< Banana Culture Entertainment>

\<EXO 엑소\>

\<Meaning: EXOPLANET\>
\<Debut: 2012\> \<Company: SM Entertainment\>
\<Official Page: exo.smtown.com\>
\<Official Weibo: www.weibo.com/exok, www.weibo.com/exom\>
\<V Live: www.vlive.tv/channels/F948D\> \<Twitter: smtownexok \>
\<Facebook: www.facebook.com/exok, www.facebook.com/exom\>
\<YouTube: www.youtube.com/EXOK, www.youtube.com/EXOM\>
\<Instagram: exok.smtown, exom.smtown \>
\<Fan Club Name: "EXO-L"\>

Stage Name: 수호 Suho
Full Name: 김준면 (Kim Jun Myun)
Birth Date: 1991.05.22
Birth Place: Seoul, South Korea
Role: Leader, Lead Vocalist
Height: 173cm/65kg
Bloodtype: AB
Zodiac Sign: Gemini
Chinese Zodiac Sign: Sheep
Facebook Fan Page: www.facebook.com/
SuHo.SMentEXO

Stage Name: 시우민 Xiumin
Full Name: 김민석 (Kim Min Seok)
Birth Date: 1990.03.26
Birth Place: Guri, South Korea
Role: Lead Vocalist, Lead Dancer
Height: 173cm/65kg
Bloodtype: B
Zodiac Sign: Aries
Chinese Zodiac Sign: Horse
Instagram: exoxm90
Facebook Fan Page: www.facebook.com/
XiuMin.Exo/

Stage Name: 레이 Lay
Full Name: Zhang Yixing
Birth Date: 1991.10.07
Birth Place: Seongnam, South Korea
Role: Main Dancer, Vocalist
Height: 177cm/60kg
Bloodtype: A
Zodiac Sign: Libra
Chinese Zodiac Sign: Sheep
Instagram: zyxzjs
Facebook Fan Page: www.facebook.com/
Lay.EXO

Stage Name: 백현 Baekhyun
Full Name: 변백현 (Byun Baekhyun)
Birth Date: 1992.05.06
Birth Place: Bucheon, South Korea
Role: Main Vocalist
Height: 174cm/58kg
Bloodtype: O
Zodiac Sign: Taurus
Chinese Zodiac Sign: Monkey
Instagram: baekhyunee_exo
Facebook Fan Page: www.facebook.com/
Solji-EXID-276684109113958

\<EXO 엑소\>

Stage Name: 첸 Chen
Full Name: 김종대 (Kim Jong Dae)
Birth Date: 1992.09.21
Birth Place: Siheung, South Korea
Role: Main Vocalist
Height: 173cm/64kg
Bloodtype: B
Zodiac Sign: Virgo
Chinese Zodiac Sign: Monkey
Instagram: kimmjongdae
Facebook Fan Page: www.facebook.com/
CHEN.EXO

Stage Name: 찬열 Chanyeol
Full Name: 박찬열 (Park Chan Yeol)
Birth Date: 1992.11.27
Birth Place: Seongnam, South Korea
Role: Main Rapper, Vocalist
Height: 185cm/70kg
Bloodtype: A
Zodiac Sign: Sagittarius
Chinese Zodiac Sign: Monkey
Instagram: real__pcy
Facebook Fan Page: www.facebook.com/
ChanYeol.SMentEXO

Stage Name: 디오 D.O.
Full Name: 도경수 (Do Kyung Soo)
Birth Date: 1993.01.12
Birth Place: Goyang, South Korea
Role: Main Vocalist
Height: 173cm/60kg
Bloodtype: A
Zodiac Sign: Capricorn
Chinese Zodiac Sign: Rooster
Instagram: kyungexok
Facebook Fan Page: www.facebook.com/
DO.SMentEXO

Stage Name: 카이 Kai
Full Name: 김종인 (Kim Jong In)
Birth Date: 1994.01.14
Birth Place: Suncheon, South Korea
Role: Leader, Main Dancer, Vocalist, Lead
Rapper, Visual
Height: 182cm/65kg
Bloodtype: A
Zodiac Sign: Capricorn
Chinese Zodiac Sign: Rooster
Instagram: kimkaaaaaa
Facebook Fan Page: www.facebook.com/
KAI.EXO

Stage Name: 세훈 Sehun
Full Name: 오세훈 (Oh Se Hun)
Birth Date: 1994.04.12
Birth Place: Seoul, South Korea
Role: Lead Dancer, Rapper, Sub-Vocalist,
Maknae
Height: 183cm/63kg
Bloodtype: O
Zodiac Sign: Aries
Chinese Zodiac Sign: Dog
Instagram:oohsehun
Facebook Fan Page: www.facebook.com/
SeHun.EXO

★SUB UNITS★

EXO-M (Mandarin)
Tao*, Kris*, Luhan*, Lay, Chen, Xiu Min
*Left Group

EXO-K (Korean)
Suho, Kai, Se Hun, D.O, Baek Hyun,
Chanyeol

EXO-CBX
Chen, Baekhyun and Xiumin

‹EXO 엑소›

★WORKS★

Full Albums
2013: XOXO
2015: Exodus
2016: Ex'Act

Single Albums
2012: What is Love, History, Mama
2013: Wolf, Growl, Miracles in December
2014: 2014: Overdose, December, 2014 (The Winter's Tale)
2015: Call Me Baby, Love Me Right, Lightsaber, Sing for You, Unfair
Love Me Right ~romantic universe~ (Japanese)
2016: Monster, Lucky One, Lotto, Dancing King, For Life
Coming Over (Japanese)

★FILMOGRAPHY★

2012: To the Beautiful You (SBS)
2013: Exo's Showtime (MBC every1), Weekly Idol Ep. 103, 108 (MBC every1), A Song For You Ep. 1-2 (KBS), Running Man Ep.171-172 (SBS), Infinite Challenge Ep. 345 (MBC)
2014: XOXO EXO (Mnet), EXO 90:2014 (Mnet), Infinite Challenge Ep. 366 (MBC)
2015: SurpLINEs EXO (Line TV), EXO Channel (TV Tokyo), EXO Next Door (Naver TV Cast), Yoo Hee Yeol's Sketchbook Ep. 277 (KBS), Infinite Challenge Ep. 424 (MBC)
2016: KBS MV Bank Stardust Ep. 49 (KBS), Infinite Challenge Ep.498 (MBC), Star Show 360 Ep. 1,2 (MBC every1)

★TOURS/CONCERTS★

2014-2015: Exo from Exoplanet #1 - The Lost Planet
2015-2016: Exo Planet #2 - The Exo'luxion
2016-2017: Exo Planet #3 - The Exo'rdium

★AWARDS★

2012: B est New Asian Artist Group, BC - UnionPay Album of the Year - "XOXO ((Mnet Asian Music Awards)
2013: Newcomer Award - EXO-K (Golden Disk Awards)
2013: New Artist Award (Seoul Music Awards)
2013: Group Musician of the Year by Netizen Vote (Korean Music Awards)
2013: Netizen Popularity Award, Top 10 Artists, Song of the Year - "Growl" (MelOn Music Awards)
2014: Disk Daesang - "XOXO" (Golden Disk Awards)
2014: Best Dance & Electronic Song - "Growl" (Korean Music Awards)
2014: Top 10 Artists (MelOn Music Awards)
2014: Popularity Award, Artist of the Year - "XOXO", "Miracles in December" (Gaon Chart K-Pop Awards)
2014: Bonsang Award, Daesang Award (Seoul Music Awards)
2015: Disk Bonsang, Disk Daesang - "Overdose" (Golden Disk Awards)
2015: Top 10 Artists, Album of the Year - "EXODUS" (MelOn Music Awards)
2015: Best Male Group, Weibo - Global Fan's Choice Male Group, Best Asian Style Award (Mnet Asian Music Awards)
2015: Popularity Award, Artist of the Year - "Overdose" (Gaon Chart K-Pop Awards)
2015: Bonsang Award, iQiyi Popularity Award, Daesang Award (Seoul Music Awards)
2016: Daesang Award (Singer), Asia Star Award, Popularity Award, Baidu Star Award (Asia Artist Awards)
2016: Global Popularity Award, Disk Bonsang, Disk Daesang - "EXODUS" (Golden

Disk Awards)
2016: Artist of the Year, Top 10 Artists, Netizen
Popularity Award, Kakao Hot Star Award, Best
Male Dance - "Monster" (MelOn Music Awards)

"Love Me Right ~romantic universe~"
2015.11.18
<SM Entertainment>

<f(x) 에프엑스>

<Meaning: Flower + Unique talents and charms through music>
<Debut: 2009> <Company: SM Entertainment>
<Official Page: fx.smtown.com>
<V Live: www.vlive.tv/channels/FD53B> <Fan Twitter: AffxtionGlobal >
<Facebook: www.facebook.com/fx.smtown>
<YouTube: www.youtube.com/user/fxsmtown>
<Fan Club Name: "MeU">

Stage Name: 빅토리아 Victoria
Full Name: 빅토리아 송 (Victoria Song)
Birth Date: 1987.02.02
Birth Place: Shandong, China
Role: Leader, Main Dancer, Vocalist
Height: 168cm
Bloodtype: A
Zodiac Sign: Aquarius
Chinese Zodiac Sign: Rabbit
Instagram: victoria02_02
Facebook Fan Page: www.facebook.com/
fx.victoriaqiannie

———————————————

Stage Name: 앰버 Amber
Full Name: Amber Josephine Liu
Birth Date: 1992.09.18
Birth Place: California, United States
Role: Main Rapper, Sub Vocalist
Height: 167 cm
Bloodtype: B
Zodiac Sign: Virgo
Chinese Zodiac Sign: Monkey
Instagram: ajol_llama
Twitter: llama_ajol
Facebook Fan Page: www.facebook.com/
fx.amberjosephineliu

———————————————

Stage Name: 루나 Luna
Full Name: 박선영 (Park Sun Young)
Birth Date: 1993.08.12
Birth Place: Seoul, South Korea
Role: Main Vocalist, Lead Dancer
Height: 161cm
Bloodtype: A
Zodiac Sign: Leo
Chinese Zodiac Sign: Rooster
Instagram: HERMOSAVIDALUNA
Facebook Fan Page: www.facebook.com/
fx-Luna-122691487683

———————————————

Stage Name: 크리스탈 Krystal
Full Name: 정수정 (Jung Soo Jung)
Birth Date: 1994.10.24
Birth Place: California, United States
Role: Lead Vocalist, Maknae
Height: 165cm
Bloodtype: A
Zodiac Sign: Scorpio
Chinese Zodiac Sign: Monkey
Instagram: vousmevoyez
Facebook Fan Page: www.facebook.com/
KrystalJungSooJung

———————————————

‹f(x) 에프엑스›

★WORKS★

Full Albums
2011: Pinocchio
2013: Pink Tape
2014: Red Light
2015: 4 Walls

Single Albums
2009: La Cha Ta, Chocolate Love, Chu
2010: Nu ABO, Mr. Boogie, Lollipop (Chinese)
2011: Pinocchio (Danger), Hot Summer
2012: Electric Shock, Hot Summer (Japanese)
2013: Rum Pum Pum Pum 2014: Red Light
2015: 4 Walls, Wish List, Pinocchio (Japanese)
2016: All Line, 4 Walls/Cowboy (Japanese)

★FILMOGRAPHY★
2012: To the Beautiful You (SBS)
2013: Exo's Showtime (MBC every1), Weekly Idol Ep. 103, 108 (MBC every1), A Song For You Ep. 1-2 (KBS), Running Man Ep.171-172 (SBS), Infinite Challenge Ep. 345 (MBC)
2014: XOXO EXO (Mnet), EXO 90:2014 (Mnet), Infinite Challenge Ep. 366 (MBC)
2015: SurpLINEs EXO (Line TV), EXO Channel (TV Tokyo), EXO Next Door (Naver TV Cast), Yoo Hee Yeol's Sketchbook Ep. 277 (KBS), Infinite Challenge Ep. 424 (MBC)
2016: KBS MV Bank Stardust Ep. 49 (KBS), Infinite Challenge Ep.498 (MBC), Star Show 360 Ep. 1,2 (MBC every1)

★TOURS/CONCERTS★
2016: Dimension 4 - Docking Station

Participation
2010-2011: SM Town Live '10 World Tour
2012-2013: SM Town Live World Tour III
2013: SM Town Week (with EXO)
2014-2015: SM Town Live World Tour IV
2016: SM Town Live World Tour V

★AWARDS★
2009: Best New Artist (Bugs Music Awards), Rookie of the Month (Cyworld Digital Music Awards), Best New Female Artists - "La Cha Ta" (Mnet Asian Music Awards)
2010: Rookie Singer Award (Korean Entertainment Arts Awards)
2011: Music Video of the Year - "Pinocchio (Danger)" (Bugs Music Awards), Group/Musician of the Year Netizen Vote (Korean Music Awards), Top 10 Artist Winners (Bonsang) (MelOn Music Awards), Hot Blue Carpet Star, Hot Trend Musician (Mnet 20's Choice Awards)
2012: Disk Bonsang - "Pinocchio (Danger)" (Golden Disk Awards), Best Dance Performance - Female Group (Mnet Asian Music Awards), Best Group Female (SBS MTV Best of the Best)
2013: Digital Bonsang - "Electric Shock", Group Singer Award (Korean Entertainment Arts Awards), Best Dance & Electronic Song - "Electric Shock" (Korean Music Awards), MBC Music Star Award (MelOn Music Awards), Bonsang Award - "Electric Shock" (Seoul Music Awards)
2014: Disk Bonsang - "Pink Tape" (Golden Disk Awards), Group Singer Award (Korean Entertainment Arts Awards)
2015: Global Choice Female Group (Mnet Asian Music Awards)
2016: Disk Bonsang - "4 Walls" (Golden Disk Awards), Awesome Wannabe (Style Icon Asia)

"Red Light"
2014.07.07
\<SM Entertainment\>

<FT ISLAND>
<에프티 아일랜드>

<Meaning: Five Treasure Island>
<Debut: 2007> <Company: FNC Entertainment>
<Official Page: fncent.com/FTISLAND>
<Official Weibo: weibo.com/ftislandofficial>
<V Live: www.vlive.tv/channels/FE913>
<Facebook: www.facebook.com/ftisland>
<YouTube: www.youtube.com/ftisland>
<Fan Club Name: "Primadonna">

Stage Name: 종훈 Jonghun
Full Name: 최종훈 (Choi Jong Hoon)
Birth Date: 1990.03.07
Birth Place: Seoul, South Korea
Role: Leader, Guitarist, Piano & Bassist
Height: 178cm/61kg
Bloodtype: A
Zodiac Sign: Pisces
Chinese Zodiac Sign: Horse
Instagram: ftgtjhc
Twitter: FtGtJH

Stage Name: 홍기 Hongki
Full Name: 이홍기 (Lee Hong Ki)
Birth Date: 1990.03.02
Birth Place: Seoul, South Korea
Role: Lead Vocalist, Visual
Height: 176cm/60kg
Bloodtype: AB
Zodiac Sign: Pisces
Chinese Zodiac Sign: Horse
Instagram: skullhong12
Twitter: skullhong
Facebook Fan Page: www.facebook.com/
Lee-Hong-Ki-163867013650836

Stage Name: 재진 Jaejin
Full Name: 이재진 (Lee Jae Jin)
Birth Date: 1991.12.17
Birth Place: Cheongju, South Korea
Role: Bassist, Lead Vocalist
Height: 177cm/58kg
Bloodtype: A
Zodiac Sign: Sagittarius
Chinese Zodiac Sign: Sheep
Instagram: saico0111
Twitter: saicowow

Stage Name: 민환 Minhwan
Full Name: 최민환 (Choi Min Hwan)
Birth Date: 1992.11.11
Birth Place: Seoul, South Korea
Role: Drummer and Maknae
Height: 171cm/62kg
Bloodtype: A
Zodiac Sign: Scorpio
Chinese Zodiac Sign: Monkey
Instagram: minhwan12
Twitter: FtDrMH1111

\<FT ISLAND\>
\<에프티 아일랜드\>

Stage Name: 승현 Seunghyun
Full Name: 송승현 (Song Seung Hyun)
Birth Date: 1992.08.21
Birth Place: Seoul, South Korea
Role: Main Rapper, Vocalist, Guitarist
Height: 181cm/65.7kg
Bloodtype: O
Zodiac Sign: Leo
Chinese Zodiac Sign: Monkey
Instagram: soow456
Twitter: chungxuan

_____

★WORKS★
2007: Cheerful Sensibility
2008: Colorful Sensibility
2009: Cross & Change
2009: So Long, Au Revoir (Japanese)
2011: Five Treasure Island (Japanese)
2012: Five Treasure Box
2012: 20 [Twenty] (Japanese)
2013: Rated-FT (Japanese)
2014: New Page (Japanese)
2015: 5.....Go (Japanese)
2015: I Will
2016: Where's the Truth?
2016: N.W.U (Japanese)

★FILMOGRAPHY★
2013-2014: Cheongdam-dong 111 (tvN)
2015: Coming Out FTISLAND (MTV)

★TOURS/CONCERTS★
Asia (Bangkok, Taipei, Shanghai, Kuala Lumpur, Hong Kong, Singapore, Beijing, Guangzhou)
2012: Play! F.T. Island
2013: Take F.T. Island Concert
2015: We Will Asia Tour
2016-17: F.T. Island Live [The Truth]

Japan
2012: F.T. Island Summer Arena Tour Run!Run!Run!
2013: F.T. Island Arena Tour FREEDOM
2014: F.T. Island Autumn Tour TO THE LIGHT
2014: F.T. Island Arena Tour THE PASSION
2015: 5th Anniversary Autumn Tour WHERE'S MY PUPPY
2016: F.T. Island Arena Tour LAW of FTISLAND: NWU
2016: F.T. Island Autumn Tour WE JUST DO IT

Europe
2015: FTHX EUROPE & LATIN Americas Tour (Paris, Santiago, Mexico City, New York, Los Angeles)

★AWARDS★
2007: Blistex's World's Most Beautiful Lips Award, Best New Asian Artist (Asia Song Festival), Popularity Award, New Comer Award (Golden Disk Awards)
2008: Newcomer Award - "Love Sick" (Seoul Music Awards, Asia's Most Popular Artist Award (SEED Awards, Thailand), Best Male Group (Korea Entertainment Arts Awards), YEPP Popularity Award (Golden Disk Awards)
2009: Teen Musical Artist Award (Korean Cultural Entertainment Awards), Hallyu Tourism Lifetime Achievement Award (Hallyu Tourism Night, Korea National Tourism Organization)
2010: Male Singer Award (Korea Entertainment Arts Awards), Cosmopolitan Rock Music Award (Golden Disk Awards)
2011: Bonsang Award (Seoul Music Awards), King Singer Award (MBC idol Star 7080), Cosmopolitan 'Fun & Fearless Musician' Award, Best Rock Musician of the Year (Golden Disk Awards)

TOP 30 Hottest KPOP Idol Bands

‹FT ISLAND›
‹에프티 아일랜드›

2012: Bonsang Award (Seoul Music Awards)
2013: Disk Bonsang (Golden Disk Awards)
2015: Asia's Popular Brand Award

"[Where`s the truth?]"
2016.07.18
‹FNC Entertainment›

"Cross & Change"
2009.07.16
‹FNC Entertainment›

<Got 7 갓세븐>

<Meaning: 7 People With Good Luck>
<Debut: 2014> <Company: JYP Entertainment>
<Official Page: got7.jype.com>
<Official Weibo: www.weibo.com/JYPEGOT7>
<V Live: www.vlive.tv/channels/ECDF> <Twitter: got7official>
<Facebook: www.facebook.com/GOT7Official>
<YouTube: www.youtube.com/c/got7>
<Fan Club Name: "GOT7">

Stage Name: 제이비 JB
Full Name: 임재범 (Im Jae Bum)
Birth Date: 1994.01.06
Birth Place: Seoul, South Korea
Role: Leader, Main Vocalist, Lead Dancer, Visual
Height: 179cm / 63kg
Bloodtype: A
Zodiac Sign: Capricorn
Chinese Zodiac Sign: Rooster
Instagram: defjeffb
Twitter: jbjyp
Facebook Fan Page: www.facebook.com/JBjyp.net

———————————————

Stage Name: 마크 Mark
Full Name: Mark Tuan (Tuan Yi Eun)
Birth Date: 1993.09.04
Birth Place: California, USA
Role: Main Rapper, Vocalist, Visual
Height: 174cm / 63kg
Bloodtype: O
Zodiac Sign: Virgo
Chinese Zodiac Sign: Rooster
Instagram: mark_tuan
Twitter: mtuan93
Facebook Fan Page: www.facebook.com/MARK.GOT7

———————————————

Stage Name: 잭슨 Jackson
Full Name: Jackson Wang (Wang Ka Yee)
Birth Date: 1994.03.28
Birth Place: Hong Kong
Role: Leader, Lead Rapper, Vocalist
Height: 174cm / 63kg
Bloodtype: O
Zodiac Sign: Capricorn
Chinese Zodiac Sign: Dog
Instagram: jacksonwang852g7
Facebook Fan Page: www.facebook.com/Official.JacksonWang

———————————————

Stage Name: 진영 Jinyoung (a.k.a Jr.)
Full Name: 박진영 (Park Jin Young)
Birth Date: 1994.09.22
Birth Place: Jinhae, South Korea
Role:Lead Vocalist, Lead Dancer, Rapper
Height: 178cm / 63kg
Bloodtype: O
Zodiac Sign: Virgo
Chinese Zodiac Sign: Dog
Instagram: pepi_jy
Twitter: jrjyp
Facebook Fan Page: www.facebook.com/JRjyp.net

———————————————

<Got 7 갓세븐>

Stage Name: 영재 Youngjae
Full Name: 최영재 (Choi Young Jae)
Birth Date: 1996.09.17
Birth Place: Shandong, China
Role: Leader, Main Dancer, Vocalist
Height: 177cm / 61kg
Bloodtype: B
Zodiac Sign: Virgo
Chinese Zodiac Sign: Rat
Instagram: 333cyj333
Twitter: GOTYJ_Ars_Vita
Facebook Fan Page: www.facebook.com/
cyj1996.09.17

Stage Name: 뱀뱀 BamBam
Full Name: Kunpimook Bhuwakul
Birth Date: 1997.05.02
Birth Place: Bangkok, Thailand
Role: Lead Rapper, Vocalist
Height: 174.5cm / 52kg
Bloodtype: B
Zodiac Sign: Taurus
Chinese Zodiac Sign: Ox
Instagram: bambam1a
Twitter: BamBam1A
Facebook Fan Page: www.facebook.com/
bambam.GOT7

Stage Name: 유겸 Yugyeom
Full Name: 김유겸 (Kim Yu Gyeom)
Birth Date: 1997.11.17
Birth Place: Namyangju, South Korea
Role: Lead Dancer, Vocalist, Maknae
Height: 180cm / 64kg
Bloodtype: A
Zodiac Sign: Scorpio
Chinese Zodiac Sign: Ox
Instagram: yu_gyeom
Facebook Fan Page: www.facebook.com/
KimYugyeomOfficialFanpage

★WORKS★

2014: Identity
2016: Flight Log: Turbulence
2016: Moriagatteyo (Japanese)

Singles
2014: Girls, Girls, Girls, A, Stop Stop It /
Around the World (Japanese)
2015: Just Right, If You Do, Fly, Love / Train,
Laugh, Laugh, Laugh (Japanese)
2016: Home Run, Hard Carry / Yo Morigatte
Yo, Hey Yah (Japanese)

★FILMOGRAPHY★

2012: Dream High 2 (KBS2)
2013: When a Man Falls in Love (MBC)
2015: Dream Knight (Line TV), Beloved
Eun-Dong (JTBC)
2016: Jealousy Incarnate, The Legend of the
Blue Sea (SBS)
2017: Nunbal (Flurry of Snow), Movie

★TOURS/CONCERTS★

2014: Got7 Japan Tour : "Around The World"
2016: Got 7 Japan Tour

World Tour
2016: Fly Tour (South Korea, China, Japan,
Thailand, United States - Dallas, Chicago,
New York, Atlanta, LA)

★AWARDS★

2014: Best New Artist (SBS MTV Best of
the Best)
2015: Best New Artist (Golden Disk
Awards), Rookie Award (Seoul Music
Awards), Chinese Netizen Popularity Award
(SBS Awards Festival), Asia Style Best
Influence Group (Fashion Power Awards)

<Got 7 갓세븐>

2016: Best Performance Boy Group - "Fly"
(Simply K-Pop Awards), iQiYi Worldwide Favorite Artist (Mnet Asian Music Awards), Disk
Bonsang - "Flight Log: Turbulence" (Golden
Disk Awards), Best Male Group (SBS PopAsia
Awards)
2017: Bonsang Award - "Flight Log: Turbulence"
(Seoul Music Awards)

"Moriagatteyo"
2016.08.04
<JYP Entertainment>

\<INFINITE 인피니트\>

\<Meaning: Limitless\>
\<Debut: 2010\> \<Company: Woolim Entertainment\>
\<Official Page: www.ifnt7.com\> \<Official Weibo: www.weibo.com/officialifnt\>
\<V Live: www.vlive.tv/channels/FE815\> \<Twitter: Official_IFNT\>
\<Facebook: www.facebook.com/ifnt7\> \<Instagram: official_ifnt_\>
\<YouTube: www.youtube.com/user/woolliment\>
\<Fan Club Name: "Inspirit"\>

Stage Name: 성규 Sunggyu
Full Name: 김성규 (Kim Sung Gyu)
Birth Date: 1989.04.28
Birth Place: Jeonju, South Korea
Role: Main Vocalist, Leader
Height: 178cm
Bloodtype: A
Zodiac Sign: Taurus
Chinese Zodiac Sign: Snake
Instagram: gyu357
Twitter: kyuzizi
Facebook Fan Page: www.facebook.com/
SungGyu-Infinite-164619013629862

Stage Name: 동우 Dongwoo
Full Name: 장동우 (Jang Dong Woo)
Birth Date: 1990.11.22
Birth Place: Gyeonggi, South Korea
Role: Main Rapper, Lead Dancer, Vocalist
Height: 175cm
Bloodtype: A
Zodiac Sign: Sagittarius
Chinese Zodiac Sign: Horse
Instagram: ddong_gg0
Twitter: ddww1122 Facebook
Fan Page: www.facebook.com/
AlwaysHappyDino

Stage Name: 우현 WooHyun
Full Name: 남우현 (Nam Woo Hyun)
Birth Date: 1991.02.08
Birth Place: ChungCheong, South Korea
Role: Main Vocalist
Height: 176cm
Bloodtype: B
Zodiac Sign: Aquarius
Chinese Zodiac Sign: Sheep
Instagram: nwh91
Twitter: wowwh
Facebook Fan Page: www.facebook.com/
NamHeartKing

Stage Name: 호야 Hoya
Full Name: 이호원 (Lee Ho Won)
Birth Date: 1991.03.28
Birth Place: Busan, South Korea
Role: Lead Rapper, Main Dancer, Vocalist
Height: 178cm
Bloodtype: AB
Zodiac Sign: Aries
Chinese Zodiac Sign: Sheep
Instagram: isayhousayya
Twitter: hoya1991
Facebook Fan Page: www.facebook.com/
TheDancingMachineHoBaby

\<INFINITE 인피니트\>

Stage Name: 성열 Sungyeol
Full Name: 이성열 (Lee Sung Yeol)
Birth Date: 1991.08.27
Birth Place: Gyeonggi, South Korea
Role: Vocalist
Height: 183cm
Bloodtype: B
Zodiac Sign: Virgo
Chinese Zodiac Sign: Sheep
Instagram: leeseongyeol_1991
Twitter: Seongyeol1991
Facebook Fan Page: www.facebook.com/
JBjyp.net

Stage Name: 엘/명수 L/Myungsoo
Full Name: 김명수 (Kim Myung Soo)
Birth Date: 1992.03.13
Birth Place: Seoul, South Korea
Role: Vocalist, Visual
Height: 180cm
Bloodtype: O
Zodiac Sign: Pisces
Chinese Zodiac Sign: Monkey
Instagram: kim_msl
Twitter: INFINITELKIM
Facebook Fan Page: www.facebook.com/
Myungsoo.L.OfInfinite

Stage Name: 성종 Sungjong
Full Name: 이성종 (Lee Sung Jong)
Birth Date: 1993.03.13
Birth Place: Gwangju, South Korea
Role: Vocalist, Maknae
Height: 179cm
Bloodtype: A
Zodiac Sign: Virgo
Chinese Zodiac Sign: Rooster
Instagram: ssongjjong.ifnt
Twitter: infiniteyounges
Facebook Fan Page: www.facebook.com/

Stage Name: 성열 Sungyeol
Full Name: 이성열 (Lee Sung Yeol)
Birth Date: 1991.08.27
Birth Place: Gyeonggi, South Korea
Role: Vocalist
Height: 183cm
Bloodtype: B
Zodiac Sign: Virgo
Chinese Zodiac Sign: Sheep
Instagram: leeseongyeol_1991
Twitter: Seongyeol1991
Facebook Fan Page: www.facebook.com/
JBjyp.net

Stage Name: 엘/명수 L/Myungsoo
Full Name: 김명수 (Kim Myung Soo)
Birth Date: 1992.03.13
Birth Place: Seoul, South Korea
Role: Vocalist, Visual
Height: 180cm
Bloodtype: O
Zodiac Sign: Pisces
Chinese Zodiac Sign: Monkey
Instagram: kim_msl
Twitter: INFINITELKIM
Facebook Fan Page: www.facebook.com/
Myungsoo.L.OfInfinite

Stage Name: 성종 Sungjong
Full Name: 이성종 (Lee Sung Jong)
Birth Date: 1993.03.13
Birth Place: Gwangju, South Korea
Role: Vocalist, Maknae
Height: 179cm
Bloodtype: A
Zodiac Sign: Virgo
Chinese Zodiac Sign: Rooster
Instagram: ssongjjong.ifnt
Twitter: infiniteyounges
Facebook Fan Page: www.facebook.com/

\<INFINITE 인피니트\>

SungjongBabyMaknae

★UNIT BREAKDOWN★
Infinite H - Dongwoo & Hoya
Infinite F - Sungyeol, L, Sungjong

★WORKS★
2011: Over the Top
2013: Koi ni Ochiru Toki (Japanese)
2014: Season 2
2015: For You (Japanese)

★FILMOGRAPHY★
2010: You're My Oppa (Mnet), Children of the Night Ep. 1-4 (MBC)
2011: Warawara Store (Tooniverse), Infinite Sesame Player (Mnet), Weekly Idol Ep. 4, 23 (MBC), Birth of a Family Ep. 1-10, 12 (KBS2)
2012: Infinite Concert: Second Invasion Evolution the Movie 3D (Movie), Infinite Ranking King (Mnet), Weekly Idol Ep. 47,48,56 (MBC)
2013: Lee Soo Geun and Kim Byung Man's High Society Ep. 45-47 (JTBC), Infinity Challenge Ep.341-342 (MBC)
2014: Grow: Infinite's Real Youth Life (Movie), Running Man Ep. 179,180,201 (SBS), After School Club (Arirang TV), Hi! School: Love On (KBS)
2015: You Hee-yeol's Sketchbook Ep. 253 (KBS2), A Song For You 4 Ep. 4 (KBS)
2016: Infinite Showtime Ep. 1-12 (MBC every1), You Hee-Yeol's Sketchbook Ep. 337 (KBS 2), Weekly Idol Ep. 269 (MBC every1), After School Club (Arirang TV), Knowing Bros Ep. 46 (JTBC), SNL Korea S8 Ep.8 (tvN)

★TOURS/CONCERTS★
World
2013-2014: Infinite 1st World Tour "One Great Step"
2015-2016: 2015 Infinite 2nd World Tour "INFINITE EFFECT"

Asia
2017: Asia Fan Meeting Tour 2017 "Infinite Only Show"

Korea
2012: Infinite Second Invasion
2012: 2012 Infinite Concert: That Summer
2014: Infinite Concert: That Summer 2
2016: Infinite Concert: That Summer

Japan
2011: Infinite Japan 1st Live - Leaping Over
2012: Infinite 1st Arena Tour in Japan - Second Invasion Evolution Plus
2015: Infinite Japan Tour - DILEMMA
Infinite Japan Tour: That Summer 3 (2016)

★AWARDS★
2012: Disk Bonsang Award - "Over the Top", Hallyu Icon Award (Golden Disk Awards), Group Musician of the Year by Netizens - "Over the Top" (Korean Music Awards), 2012 Top 10 (MelOn Music Awards)
2013: Disk Bonsang Award, Best Group Performance (Golden Disk Awards), Best Male Group, Sony MDR World Wide Performer (Mnet Asian Music Awards)2014: Disk Bonsang Award - "New Challenge" (Golden Disk Awards), Bonsang Award (Seoul Music Awards), K-Pop Fan's Choice - Male (Mnet Asian Music Awards)
2015: Disk Bonsang Award - "Season 2" (Golden Disk Awards), Bonsang Award, Special Hallyu Award (Seoul Music Awards), Group Musician of the Year by Netizen - "Season 2" (Korean Music Awards)

<INFINITE 인피니트>

2016: Best Singer (Korea Cable TV Awards), Most Popular Artists (Singer) - Top 50 (Asia Artist Awards), Top Singer Award (The Night of Stars-Korea Top Star Awards)

"Over the Top" 2011.07.21
< Woolim Entertainment>

"Season 2" 2014.05.21
< Woolim Entertainment>

TOP 30 Hottest KPOP Idol Bands

‹MAMAMOO 마마무›

‹Meaning: "MAMA (Mother) + Moo (Sound Babies Make) = Organic/Instinctive Music"› ‹Debut: 2014› ‹Company: RBW Entertainment›
‹Official Page: rbbridge.com/pages/artist1›
‹Weibo: WAMAMAMOO›
‹V Live: channels.vlive.tv/FCD4B›
‹Facebook: www.facebook.com/RBW.MAMAMOO›
‹Instagram: mamamoo_official›
‹YouTube: www.youtube.com/user/WAMamamoo›
International Fan Site ‹http://fmamamamoo.wordpress.com›

Stage Name: 솔라 Solar
Full Name: 김영선 (Kim Young Sun)
Birth Date: 1991.02.21
Birth Place: Seoul, South Korea
Role: Leader, Main Vocalist
Height: 163cm / 45kg
Bloodtype: B
Zodiac Sign: Pisces
Chinese Zodiac Sign: Sheep

_____

Stage Name: 문별 Moonbyul
Full Name: 문별이 (Moon Byul Yi)
Birth Date: 1992.12.22
Birth Place: Bucheon, South Korea
Role: Main Rapper, Main Dancer
Height: 165cm / 45kg
Bloodtype: B
Zodiac Sign: Sagittarius
Chinese Zodiac Sign: Monkey
Facebook Fan Page: www.facebook.com/
loveformoonbyul

_____

Stage Name: 휘인 Wheein
Full Name: 정휘인 (Whee In)
Birth Date: 1995.04.17
Birth Place: Jeonju, South Korea
Role: Lead Vocalist, Lead Dancer
Height: 162cm / 43kg
Bloodtype: B

Zodiac Sign: Capricorn
Chinese Zodiac Sign: Pig
Facebook Fan Page: www.facebook.com/
MMMOOWheein

_____

Stage Name: 화사 Hwa Sa
Full Name: 안혜진 (Ahn Hye Jin)
Birth Date: 1995.07.23
Birth Place: Jeonju, South Korea
Role: Lead Vocalist, Lead Rapper, Maknae
Height: 162cm / 44kg
Bloodtype: A
Zodiac Sign: Leo
Chinese Zodiac Sign: Pig

_____

★WORKS★

2016: Melting

Singles
2014: "Don't Be Happy", "Peppermint Chocolate", "Heeheehaheho", "Mr. Ambiguous", "Piano Man"
2015: "Ahh Oop!", "Um Oh Ah Yeh"
2016: "I Miss You", "Taller than You", "You're the Best". "New York", "Decalcomanie"

‹MAMAMOO 마마무›

★FILMOGRAPHY★

2014: Love Request Ep. 761 (KBS1), You Hee-Yeol's Sketchbook Ep. 238 (KBS2), Open Concert Ep. 1044 (KBS1)

2015: Immortal Song 2 Ep. 181, 186, 188, 193, 214, 215, 223, 224 (KBS2), Concert 7080 Ep. 494 (KBS1), Open Concert Ep. 1057 (KBS 1), Fashion King Ep. 3 (SBS Plus), Yoo Hee-Yeol's Sketchbook Ep. 281 (KBS2), After School Club Ep. 169 (Arirang TV), Show Me the Money 4 Ep. 9 (Mnet), Weekly Idol Ep. 214 (MBC every1), Idol Star Athletics Championships 10th Championship (MBC), Hidden Singer Season 4 Ep. 8 (JTBC)

2016: Idol Star Athletics Championships 11th (MBC), Immortal Songs 2 Ep. 240,249,277,283,284 (KBS2), Weekly Idol Ep. 240 (MBC every1), You Hee-Yeol's Sketchbook Ep. 309, 333, 341 (KBS2), Dream Players Ep. 1-4 (tvN), Baek Jong Won's Top 3 Chef King Ep. 31 (SBS), Open Concert Ep. 1098, 1118 (KBS1), SNL Korea S8 Ep.14 (tvN), Entourage Ep. 1 (tvN)

2017: Idol Party Ep. 6 (TV Chosun)

★TOURS/CONCERTS★

2017: MAMAMOO 1st Concert: Moosical

2017: MAMAMOO Concert "Moosical Curtain Call"

★AWARDS★

2014: New Artist of the Year (Gaon Chart K-Pop Awards), Rookie of the Year (Seoul Success Awards)

2015: Idol of the Year (Bugs Awards)

2016: Best Entertainer Award (Female Group) (Asia Artists Awards), Song of the Month - "You're the Best" (Gaon Chart K-Pop Awards), Top 10 Artists (MelOn Music Awards)

"Girl Crush (Innitia Nest OST)"
2015.09.16
‹RBW›

\<RED VELVET 레드벨벳>

<\Meaning: "Unique Concept & Great Music">
\<Debut: 2014> \<Company: SM Entertainment>
\<Official Page: redvelvet.smtown.com>
\<Weibo: BaiDuRedVelvetBar>
\<V Live: www.vlive.tv/channels/FD53B>
\<Facebook: www.facebook.com/RedVelvet>
\<Instagram: r edvelvet.smtown>
\<YouTube: www.youtube.com/RedVelvet>
International Fan Site \<http://forvelvet.com/forums>, \<www.forvelvet.com>

Stage Name: 아이린 Irene
Full Name: 배주현 (Bae Ju Hyun)
Birth Date: 1991.03.29
Birth Place: Daegu, South Korea
Role: eader, Main Rapper, Lead Dancer, Vocalist, Visual
Height: 160cm / 44kg
Bloodtype: A
Zodiac Sign: Aries
Chinese Zodiac Sign: Sheep
Facebook Fan Page: www.facebook.com/RedVelvet.Irene

Stage Name: 슬기 Seulgi
Full Name: 강슬기 (Kang Seul Gi)
Birth Date: 1994.02.10
Birth Place: Seoul, South Korea
Role: Lead Vocalist, Main Dancer
Height: 164cm / 42kg
Bloodtype: A
Zodiac Sign: Aquarius
Chinese Zodiac Sign: Dog
Facebook Fan Page: www.facebook.com/RedVelvet.Seulgi

Stage Name: 웬디 Wendy
Full Name: Wendy Son
Birth Date: 1994.02.21
Birth Place: Toronto, Canada
Role: Main Vocalist
Height: 160cm / 40kg
Bloodtype: O
Zodiac Sign: Pisces
Chinese Zodiac Sign: Horse
Facebook Fan Page: www.facebook.com/RedVelvet.Wendy

Stage Name: 조이 Joy
Full Name: 박수영 (Park Soo Young)
Birth Date: 1996.09.03
Birth Place: Seoul, South Korea
Role: Lead Rapper, Vocalist
Height: 168cm / 43kg
Bloodtype: A
Zodiac Sign: Virgo
Chinese Zodiac Sign: Rat
Facebook Fan Page: www.facebook.com/SMent.Joy

TOP 30 Hottest KPOP Idol Bands

\<RED VELVET 레드벨벳\>

Stage Name: 예리 Yeri
Full Name: 김예림 (Kim Ye Rim)
Birth Date: 1999.03.05
Birth Place: Seoul, South Korea
Role: Maknae, Rapper, Vocalist
Height: 160cm / 48kg
Bloodtype: O
Zodiac Sign: Pisces
Chinese Zodiac Sign: Rabbit
Facebook Fan Page: www.facebook.com/
Yeri.RedVelvet

★WORKS★

2015: The Red

Singles
2014: Happiness, Be Natural
2015: Automatic, Ice Cream Cake, Dumb Dumb, Wish Tree
2016: One of These Nights, Russian Roulette

★FILMOGRAPHY★

2015: Ice Cream TV (Naver), After School Club Ep. 154 (Arirang TV), Yaman TV (Mnet), Weekly Idol Ep. 217 (MBC every1), Today's Room Ep. 8,9 (Mnet), Idol Star Athletics Championships 10 (MBC), Global Request Show A Song For You 4 Ep. 12 (KBS2), We Got Married (11.20.2015) (MBC), SMTOWN The Stage (Film)
2016: Two Yoo Project - Sugar Man (JTBC), Idol Star Athletics Championships 11 (MBC), Weekly Idol Ep. 242 (MBC every1), Yoo Hee-Yeol's Sketchbook Ep. 313 (KBS2), Knowing Bros Ep. 21 (JTBC), Weekly Idol Ep. 267 (MBC every1), Yang & Nam Show Ep. 4-5, Party Idol (Mnet), Victory Ep. 1,2,5 (Naver V Live)
2017: Raid the Convenience Store Ep. 2(tvN), Idol Star Athletics Championships 12, Girl Group War - Song of Glory (KBS2)

★TOURS/CONCERTS★

2014-2015: SM Town Live World Tour IV
2014: Best Of Best in Guangzhou
2015: Best Of Best in the Philippines KCON
2015: KCON '15: Los Angeles, California
2016: SM Town Live World Tour V

★AWARDS★

2014: Best Remake Song - "Be Natural" (SBS MTV Best of the Best)
2015: Hot Performance of the Year (Gaon Chart K-Pop Awards), New Artist Award (Golden Disk Awards), Best Female Dance - "Ice Cream Cake" (MelOn Music Awards), Best Dance Performance - Female Group - "Ice Cream Cake" (Mnet Asian Music Awards), New Artist Award (Seoul Music Awards), Best Rookie Award (Korean Entertainment Arts Awards)
2016: Digital Bonsang - "Ice Cream Cake" (Golden Disk Awards), Top 10 Artists, Best Music Video - 'Russian Roulette"(MelOn Music Awards), Bonsang - "Ice Cream Cake" (Seoul Music Award), Netizen's Choice Award (Korean Entertainment Arts Awards)
2017: Bonsang - "Russian Roulette" (Seoul Music Awards), Ceci Asia Icon Award (Golden Disk Awards)

"The Red"
2015.09.09
<SM Entertainment>

"Be Natural"
2014.10.13
<SM Entertainment>

<SHINee 샤이니>

<Meaning: "One Who Receives The Light">
<Debut: 2008> <Company: SM Entertainment>
<Official Page: shinee.smtown.com>
<Weibo: www.weibo.com/baidushineebar>
<V Live: www.vlive.tv/channels/FD53B> <Twitter: shinetter>
<Facebook: www.facebook.com/shinee>
<Instagram: shinee_jp_official>
<YouTube: www.youtube.com/shinee>
<Fan Club Name: "SHINee World (a.k.a "Shawol")">

Stage Name: 온유 Onew
Full Name: 이진기 (Lee Jin Ki)
Birth Date: 1989.12.14
Birth Place: Gwangmyeong, South Korea
Role: Main Vocalist, Leader
Height: 178cm
Bloodtype: O
Zodiac Sign: Sagittarius
Chinese Zodiac Sign: Snake
Instagram: dlstmxkakwldrl
Twitter: skehehdanfdldi
Facebook Fan Page: www.facebook.com/
onewsangtae1

Stage Name: 종현 Jonghyun
Full Name: 김종현 (Kim Jong Hyun)
Birth Date: 1990.04.08
Birth Place: Seoul, South Korea
Role: Lead Vocalist
Height: 174cm
Bloodtype: AB
Zodiac Sign: Aries
Chinese Zodiac Sign: Horse
Instagram: jonghyun.948
Twitter: realjonghyun90
Facebook Fan Page: www.facebook.com/
Kim-Jonghyun-SHINee-479535045413079

Stage Name: 키 Key
Full Name: 김기범 (Kim Ki Bum)
Birth Date: 1991.09.23
Birth Place: Daegu, South Korea
Role: Vocalist, Lead Rapper
Height: 181cm
Bloodtype: B
Zodiac Sign: Virgo
Chinese Zodiac Sign: Sheep
Instagram: bumkeyk
Facebook Fan Page: www.facebook.com/
shineekimkibum

Stage Name: 민호 Minho
Full Name: 최민호 (Choi Min Ho)
Birth Date: 1991.12.09
Birth Place: Incheon, South Korea
Role: Main Rapper, Visual
Height: 184cm
Bloodtype: B
Zodiac Sign: Sagittarius
Chinese Zodiac Sign: Sheep
Facebook Fan Page: www.facebook.com/
Minho.SHINee.Intl

<SHINee 샤이니>

Stage Name: 태민 Taemin
Full Name: 이태민 (Lee Tae Min)
Birth Date: 1993.07.18
Birth Place: Seoul, South Korea
Role: Vocalist, Main Dancer, Maknae
Height: 179cm
Bloodtype: B
Zodiac Sign: Cancer
Chinese Zodiac Sign: Rooster
Instagram: gyu357
Twitter: kyuzizi
Facebook Fan Page: www.facebook.com/
Taemin-Lee-Fan-club-ShinEE-256145392085

★WORKS★
2008: The SHINee World
2010: Lucifer
2011: The First (Japanese)
2013: Dream Girl - The Misconceptions of You,
Why So Serious? - The Misconceptions of Me /
Boys Meet U (Japanese)
2014: I'm Your Boy (Japanese)
2015: Odd
2016: DxDxD (Japanese), 1 for 1
2017: Five (Japanese)

★FILMOGRAPHY★
2012: I AM (Film), World Date with SHINee
(KBS), Dear My Family (SM Town)
2013: You're The Best, Lee Soon-shin (KBS 2),
SHINee's One Fine Day (MBC)
2015: SM Town: The Stage (Film), Can You Feel
It? (D&E)

★TOURS/CONCERTS★
Asia (South Korea, Taiwan, Thailand, China,
Hong Kong, Singapore, Japan)
2010-2011: SHINee World
2012: SHINee World II

2015: SHINee World IV
2016: SHINee World V

Japan
2012: SHINee World 2012
2013: SHINee World 2013
2014: SHINee World 2014
2016: SHINee World 2016
2017: SHINee World 2017

World (South Korea, Mexico, Chile, Argentina, Taiwan, China, Indonesia)
2014: SHINee World III

★PUBLICATIONS★
2011: Children of The Sun: Onew, Key,
Taemin of SHINee in Barcelona (Woongjin
Think Big Co., Ltd ISBN 8901136058)
2013: SHINee Surprise Vacation -
Travel Note, (S.M. Entertainment ISBN
8996955434)

★AWARDS★
2008: Best New Asian Artist (Asia Song Fes-
tival), Newcomer Album of the Year - "The
SHINee World", Best Newcomer (Korean
Culture Entertainment Awards), Hot New
Star (Mnet 20's Choice Awards), Best New
Male Group (Mnet Asian Music Awards)
2009: Popularity Award (Golden Disk
Awards), Best Newcomer (Seoul Music
Award)
2010: Popularity Award, Disk Bonsang
- "Lucifer" (Golden Disk Awards), Male
Group Award (Korea Entertainment Arts
Awards), Netizens Popularity Battle Awards
- "Lucifer" (MelOn Music Awards), Bonsang
Award - "2009, Year of Us"
2011: Most Anticipated Group for 2012

<SHINee 샤이니>

(MBC Entertainment Awards), Global Star (SBS MTV Best of the Best), Bonsang - "Lucifer", Popularity Award (Seoul Music Awards)
2012: Best Male Vocalist (Korean Culture Entertainment Awards), Minister of Culture (Korean Popular Culture and Arts Awards), Best Dance Performance - Male Group (Mnet Asian Music Awards), Live Performance, Best Group Male (SBS MTV Best of the Best)
2013: Popularity Award, Disk Bonsang - "Sherlock" (Golden Disk Awards), Popularity Award (MBC Entertainment Awards), Bonsang, Artist of the Year (MelOn Music Awards), 20's Performance (Mnet 20's Choice Awards), Best Male Group (Mnet Asian Music Awards), Artist of the Year (SBS MTV Best of the Best), Bonsang Award - "Sherlock", Popularity Award (Seoul Music Awards)

2014: Ceci Asia Icon Award, Popularity Award, Disk Bonsang - "Dream Girl - The Misconceptions of You" (Golden Disk Awards), Bonsang Award - "Dream Girl - The Misconceptions of You", Popularity Award, Special Hallyu Award
2015: Bonsang (MelOn Music Awards), Best Dance Performance - Male Group (Mnet Asian Music Awards)
2016: Asia's Best Group Award (DongFang Music Awards), Popularity Award, Disk Bonsang - "Odd" (Golden Disk Awards), Prime Minister's Award (Korean Popular Culture and Arts Awards), Bonsang Award (Seoul Music Awards)
2017: Popularity Award, Disk Bonsang - "1 of 1" (Golden Disk Awards)

"I'm Your Boy"
2014.10.01
<SM Entertainment>

"1 of 1"
2016.10.05
<SM Entertainment>

\<Sistar 씨스타\>

\<Meaning: "Friendly Big Star"\>
\<Debut: 2010\> \<Company: Starship Entertainment\>
\<Official Page: www.starship-ent.com/sistar\>
\<Weibo: www.weibo.com/wearesistar\>
\<V Live: www.vlive.tv/channels/FE221\> \<Twitter: sistarsistar\>
\<Facebook: www.facebook.com/officialsistar\>
\<Instagram: official_sistar\>
\<YouTube: www.youtube.com/sistar\>
\<Fan Club Name: "Star 1"\>

Stage Name: 효린 Hyolyn
Full Name: 김효정 (Kim Hyo Jung)
Birth Date: 1991.01.11
Birth Place: Incheon, South Korea
Role: Leader, Main Vocalist, Visual
Height: 164cm / 45kg
Bloodtype: B
Zodiac Sign: Capricorn
Chinese Zodiac Sign: Horse
Instagram: xhyolynx
Facebook Fan Page: www.facebook.com/
SistarHyorinFans

Stage Name: 보라 Bora
Full Name: 윤보라 (Yoon Bo Ra)
Birth Date: 1990.01.30
Birth Place: Seoul, South Korea
Role: Main Rapper
Height: 165cm / 46kg
Bloodtype: O
Zodiac Sign: Aquarius
Chinese Zodiac Sign: Horse
Instagram: borabora_sugar
Facebook Fan Page: www.facebook.com/
Bora-sistar-128044677257907

Stage Name: 소유 Soyou
Full Name: 강지현 (Kang Ji Hyun)
Birth Date: 1992.02.12
Birth Place: Jeju Island, South Korea
Role: Sub Vocalist
Height: 168cm / 49kg
Bloodtype: O
Zodiac Sign: Aquarius
Chinese Zodiac Sign: Monkey
Instagram: soooo_you
Facebook Fan Page: www.facebook.com/
Sistar.KangSoyou

Stage Name: 다솜 Dasom
Full Name: 김다솜 (Kim Da Som)
Birth Date: 1993.05.06
Birth Place: Seoul, South Korea
Role: Vocalist, Maknae
Height: 167cm / 44kg
Bloodtype: A
Zodiac Sign: Taurus
Chinese Zodiac Sign: Rooster
Instagram: som0506
Facebook Fan Page: www.facebook.com/
sistarmaknae.dasom

<Sistar 씨스타>

★UNIT BREAKDOWN★

Sistar19: Hyolyn & Bora (2011)

★WORKS★

2011: So Cool
2013: Give It To Me

Singles
2010: Push Push, Shady Girl, How Dare You
2011: So Cool
2012: Alone, Loving You
2013: Give It To Me
2014: Touch My Body, I Swear
2015: Shake It
2016 I Like That

★FILMOGRAPHY★

2011: Sistar & Lee Teuk's Hello Baby (KBS World)
2012: Hello Counselor (KBS World) Ep. 82, Running Man (SBS) Ep. 95, Let's Go Dream Team! (KBS) S2 Ep.161
2013: Shinhwa Broadcast (JTBC) Ep. 45-46, Infinite Challenge Ep. 332, Let's Go Dream Team! (KBS) Season 2 Ep. 188, 1 Night 2 Days (KBS) Ep. 444, Immortal Songs 2 (DJ DOC and Choi Jinhee Special) (KBS), You Hee-Yeol's Sketchbook (KBS) Ep. 192, Running Man (SBS) Ep. 162, 174, Hello Counselor (KBS World) Ep. 127, Real Men (Christmas Special) (MBC)
2014: After School Club (Arirang TV) Ep. 89, Hello Counselor (KBS World) Ep. 180, Taxi Ep.180, SNL Korea (tvN) Ep. 25
2015: Sistar Showtime Ep. 1-8, You Hee-Yeol's Sketchbook (KBS) Ep. 279, Star Golden Bell (Lunar New Year Special) (KBS)
2016: Talents for Sale Ep. 7-8, You Hee-Yeol's Sketchbook (KBS) Ep.326, Knowing Bros (JTBC) Ep.32, Running Man (SBS) Ep.307, Fantastic Duo (SBS) Ep.13-14,, Star Show 360 (MBC every1) Ep. 6

★TOURS/CONCERTS★

2012: Femme Fatale
2013: Live Concert: S
2014: Live Concert: S - Hong Kong

★AWARDS★

2010: Rookie of the Month (Cyworld Digital Music Awards), Yepp Newcomer Award (Golden Disk Awards)
2011: Best Newcomer Award (Seoul Music Awards), T10 (Bonsang) (MelOn Music Awards), Best Style Icons (Korea Lifestyle Awards)
2012: Digital Bonsang - "So Cool" (Golden Disk Awards), Bonsang - "So Cool" (Seoul Music Awards), Top 10 (Bonsang) (MelOn Music Awards), 20's Sexiest Performance (Mnet 20's Choice Awards), BFG (Mnet Asian Music Awards)
2013: Digital Bonsang - "Alone", Samsung Galaxy Star Award (Golden Disk Awards), Bonsang - "Loving You", Digital Record of the Year - "Alone" (Seoul Music Awards), Top 10 (Bonsang) (MelOn Music Awards), Top 10 Style Icons (Style Icon Awards), Best Dance Performance - Female Group - "Give It To Me" (Mnet Asian Music Awards), Song of the Year - "Give It To Me" (Gaon Chart K-Pop Awards)
2014: Digital Bonsang - "Give It To Me", CeCi Asia Icon Award (Golden Disk Awards), Bonsang - "Give It To Me" (Seoul Music Awards), Top 10 (Bonsang) (MelOn Music Awards), Best Female Group (Mnet Asian Music Awards)
2015: Digital Bonsang - "Touch My Body"

<Sistar 씨스타>

(Golden Disk Awards), Bonsang - 'Touch My Body" (Seoul Music Awards), Bonsang - "Touch My Body" (Seoul Music Awards), Top 10 (Bonsang) (MelOn Music Awards)
2016: Digital Bonsang - "Shake It" (Golden Disk Awards), Bonsang - "Shake It" (Seoul Music Awards)
2017: Best Female Performance Group (Golden Disk Awards)

"So Cool"
2011.08.09
< Starship Entertainment>

"Give It To Me"
2013.06.11
< Starship Entertainment>

\<Super Junior\>
\<슈퍼주니어\>

\<Meaning: "Best In Every Field (Junior Represents Their Time as Trainees")\>
\<Debut: 2005\> \<Company: SM Entertainment\>
\<Official Page: superjunior.smtown.com\>
\<Weibo: www.weibo.com/superjunior\>
\<V Live: www.vlive.tv/channels/FD53B\>
\<Facebook: www.facebook.com/superjunior\>
\<YouTube: www.youtube.com/superjunior\>
\<Fan Club Name: "E.L.F (Everlasting Friends)"\>

Stage Name: 이특 Leeteuk
Full Name: 박정수 (Park Jung Soo)
Birth Date: 1983.07.01
Birth Place: Seoul, South Korea
Role: Leader, Vocalist and Rapper
Height: 179cm / 59kg
Bloodtype: A
Zodiac Sign: Cancer
Chinese Zodiac Sign: Pig
Instagram: special_js1004
Twitter: special1004
Cyworld: cy.cyworld.com/home/53885055
Facebook Fan Page: www.facebook.com/
Super-Junior-Leeteuk-440025319365583

Stage Name: 희철 Heechul
Full Name: 김희철 (Kim Hee Chul)
Birth Date: 1983.07.10
Birth Place: Hoengseong, South Korea
Role: Vocalist, Rapper
Height: 179cm / 60kg
Bloodtype: AB
Zodiac Sign: Cancer
Chinese Zodiac Sign: Pig
Instagram: kimheenim
Twitter: Heedictator
Facebook Fan Page: www.facebook.com/
Kim-Heechul-127215147300014

Stage Name: 예성 Yesung
Full Name: 김종운 (Kim Jong Woon)
Birth Date: 1984.08.24
Birth Place: Cheonan, South Korea
Role: Main Vocalist
Height: 178cm / 64kg
Bloodtype: AB
Zodiac Sign: Virgo
Chinese Zodiac Sign: Rat
Instagram: yesung1106
Twitter: shfly3424
Facebook Fan Page: www.facebook.com/
yesungkimjongwoonyesung

Stage Name: 강인 Kangin
Full Name: 김영운 (Kim Young Woon)
Birth Date: 1985.01.17
Birth Place: Seoul, South Korea
Role: Vocalist
Height: 178cm / 70kg
Bloodtype: O
Zodiac Sign: Capricorn
Chinese Zodiac Sign: Rat
Instagram: anginnim
Twitter: himsenkangin
Facebook Fan Page: www.facebook.com/
Super-Junior-Kangin-1438243506446425

\<Super Junior\>
\<슈퍼주니어\>

Stage Name: 려욱 Ryeowook
Full Name: 김려욱 (Kim Ryeo Wook)
Birth Date: 1987.06.21
Birth Place: Incheon, South Korea
Role: Main Vocalist
Height: 175cm / 58kg
Bloodtype: O
Zodiac Sign: Gemini
Chinese Zodiac Sign: Rabbit
Twitter: ryeong9
Facebook Fan Page: www.facebook.com/
ryeong9

Stage Name: 규현 Kyuhyun
Full Name: 조규현 (Cho Kyu Hyun)
Birth Date: 1988.02.03
Birth Place: Seoul, South Korea
Role: Lead Vocalist, Sub-Dancer, Maknae
Height: 180cm / 68kg
Bloodtype: A
Zodiac Sign: Aquarius
Chinese Zodiac Sign: Rabbit
Twitter: GaemGyu
Cyworld: cy.cyworld.com/home/25517209
Facebook Fan Page: www.facebook.com/
super-juniors-kyuhyun-132128380142515

Stage Name: 시원 Siwon
Full Name: 최시원 (Choi Si Won)
Birth Date: 1987.02.10
Birth Place: Seoul, South Korea
Role: Vocalist, Visual
Height: 185cm / 65kg
Bloodtype: B
Zodiac Sign: Aquarius
Chinese Zodiac Sign: Rabbit
Instagram: siwon1987
Twitter: siwon407
Facebook Fan Page: www.facebook.com/
cwon407

Stage Name: 은혁 Eunhyuk
Full Name: 이혁재 (Lee Hyuk Jae)
Birth Date: 1986.04.04
Birth Place: Goyang, South Korea
Role: Main Rapper, Vocalist and Main
Dancer
Height: 176cm / 58kg
Bloodtype: O
Zodiac Sign: Aries
Chinese Zodiac Sign: Tiger
Instagram: eunhyukee44
Twitter: AllRiseSilver
Facebook Fan Page: www.facebook.com/
Eunhyuk-Super-Junior-292859924062744

Stage Name: 동해 Donghae
Full Name: 이동해 (Lee Dong Hae)
Birth Date: 1986.10.15
Birth Place: Mokpo, South Korea
Role: Lead Vocalist, Lead Dancer, Rapper
Height: 176cm / 60kg
Bloodtype: A
Zodiac Sign: Libra
Chinese Zodiac Sign: Tiger
Instagram: leedonghae
Twitter: donghae861015
Facebook Fan Page: www.facebook.com/
EastSea

Stage Name: 신동 Shindong
Full Name: 신동희 (Shin Dong Hee)
Birth Date: 1985.09.28
Birth Place: Mungyeong, South Korea
Role:Lead Rapper and Lead Dancer
Height: 178cm / 90kg
Bloodtype: O
Zodiac Sign: Libra
Chinese Zodiac Sign: Ox
Instagram: earlyboysd
Twitter: ShinsFriends

<Super Junior>
<슈퍼주니어>

Stage Name: 성민 Sungmin
Full Name: 이성민 (Lee Sung Min)
Birth Date: 1986.01.01
Birth Place: Ilsan, South Korea
Role: Lead Vocalist, Lead Dancer
Height: 175cm / 57kg
Bloodtype: A
Zodiac Sign: Capricorn
Chinese Zodiac Sign: Ox
Twitter: imSMI
Facebook Fan Page: www.facebook.com/
LeeSungMin.Aegyo.King

Stage Name: 헨리 Henry
Full Name: Henry Lau (Liu Xian Hua)
Birth Date: 1989.10.11
Birth Place: Toronto, Canada
Role: Vocalist and Rapper
Height: 178cm
Zodiac Sign: Libra
Chinese Zodiac Sign: Snake
Instagram: henryl89
Twitter: henrylau89
Facebook Fan Page: www.facebook.com/
Henry-Lau-302108276542904

Stage Name: 조미 Zhoumi
Full Name: Zhou Mi
Birth Date: 1986.04.19
Birth Place: Wuhan, China
Role: Vocalist and Rapper
Zodiac Sign: Capricorn
Chinese Zodiac Sign: Tiger
Twitter: zhoumi_419
Weibo: www.weibo.com/sjmzhoumi

★UNIT BREAKDOWN★
Super Junior-K.R.Y. (Yesung, Ryewook, Kyuhyun)
Super Junior-T (Leeteuk, Heechul, Kangin, Shindong, Sungmin, Eunhyuk)
Super Junior-M (Sungmin, Eunhyuk, Siwon, Zhou Mi, Donghae, Ryeowook, Kyuhyun, Henry)
Super Junior-H (Leeteuk, Yesung, Kangin, Shindong, Sungmin, Eunhyuk)Super)
Junior-D&E (Donghae & Eunhyuk)

★WORKS★
2005: Twins
2007: Don't Don
2009: Sorry, Sorry
2010: Bonamana
2011: Mr. Simple
2012: Sexy, Free & Single
2013: Hero (Japanese)
2014: Mamacita
2015: Devil

★FILMOGRAPHY★
DVD
2006: Super Junior Boys in City Season 1. Kuala Lumpur
2008: Super Junior Boys in City Season 2. Tokyo
2010: Super Junior Boys in City Season 3. Hong Kong
2012: Super Junior Boys in City Season 4. Paris
2013: Super Junior Boys in City Season 5. Hawaii
2014: All About Super Junior ("Treasure Within Us")

\<Super Junior\>
\<슈퍼주니어\>

Film
2007: Attack on the Pin-Up Boys
2011: Super Show 3 3D
2012: I AM.
2013: Super Show 4 3D
2015: SM Town The Stage

2005-2006: Super Junior Show
2006: Super Adonis Camp, Mystery 6 (Mnet), Full House (SBonsang), Super Junior Mini-Drama (Mnet), Super Junior IPLE Unreleased Scene
2007: Idol World, Super Junior Animal Farm, Super Junior's Music Diary
2007-2008: Explorers of the Human Body (SBonsang)
2008: Idol Show (MBC every1), Unbelievable Outing (Season 3), Super Junior Unbelievable Story
2009: Human Network Super Junior's Miracle (MBC)
2010-2011: Super Junior's Foresight
2014-2015: Super Junior M's Guest House
2015: Super Junior One Fine Day

★TOURS/CONCERTS★

Asia (South Korea, China, Thailand, Japan, Singapore, Japan, Phillipines, Taiwan, Malyasia, Vietnam, Indonesia)
2008-2009: The 1st Asia Tour "Super Show"
2009-2010: The 2nd Asia Tour "Super Show 2"
2010-2011: The 3rd Asia Tour "Super Show 3"

World (South Korea, Indonesia, China, Singapore, Japan, Thailand, Taiwan, Philippines, Brazil, Argentina, Chile, Peru, Mexico, United Kingdom, Malaysia)
2011-2012: Super Junior World Tour "Super Show 4"
2013-2014: Super Junior World Tour "Super Show 5"
2014-2015: Super Junior World Tour "Super Show 6"

★AWARDS★

2006: Newcomer of the Year (Golden Disk Awards), Best New Group (Mnet Asian Music Awards), Best New Group, Mobile Popularity (Seoul Music Awards)
2007: Digital Bonsang - "Don't Don", TPL Anycall Popularity Award (Golden Disk Awards), Artist of the Year (Daesang Award), Auction Netizen Popularity, Mobile Popularity (Mnet Asian Music Awards)
2008: 2009: Digital Daesang, Digital Bonsang - "Sorry, Sorry" (Golden Disk Awards), Mobile Popularity Award, Netizen Popularity Award, Overseas Viewers Award (Mnet Asian Music Awards), Top 10 Artist Winners (Bonsang) - "Sorry, Sorry" (MelOn Music Awards)
2010: Digital Bonsang - "Bonamana", Asian Popularity Award (Golden Disk Awards), Bonsang - "Sorry, Sorry", Mobile Popularity, HSA (Seoul Music Awards)
2011: Digital Daesang, Digital Bonsang - "Mr. Simple", Popularity Award, MSN Japan Popularity Award (Golden Disk Awards), BMG, Album of the Year (Daesang Award) - "Mr. Simple" (Mnet Asian Music Awards), Artist of the Year (Album) (Gaon Chart Music Awards), Top 10 Artist Winners (Bonsang) (MelOn Music Awards)- "Mr. Simple"
2012: Digital Daesang, Digital Bonsang - "Sexy, Free, Single" (Golden Disk Awards), Best Global Group - Male, Best Line Award (Mnet Asian Music Awards), DS, Bonsang (Seoul Music Awards) - "Mr. Simple", Artist of the Year (Album) - "Sexy, Free & Single"

(Gaon Chart Music Awards)
2013: Bonsang, HSA (Seoul Music Awards)
2014: Digital Bonsang - "Mnet Asian Music Awardscita" (Golden Disk Awards), Artist of the Year - "Mnet Asian Music Awardscita",

"This is Love", Gaon Chart Weibo Kpop Star Award (Gaon Chart Music Awards)
2015: Digital Bonsang - "Devil" (Golden Disk Awards) , Bonsang - "Mnet Asian Music Awardscita" (Seoul Music Awards), Artist of the Year (Album) - "Devil" (Gaon Chart Music Awards)

"Devil / Magic
(Japanese Ver.)"
2016.02.04
<SM Entertainment>

"Hero"
2013.08.14
<SM Entertainment>

\<Teen Top 틴탑\>

\<Meaning: "Teenager Emoboy Emotion Next generation Talent Object Praise"\>
\<Debut: 2010\> \<Company: TOP Media\>
\<Official Page: www.teentop.co.kr/teentop\>
\<Weibo: weibo.com/n/TEENTOP_TOPMEDIA\>
\<V Live: www.vlive.tv/channels/FD045\> \<Twitter: TEEN_TOP\>
\<Facebook: www.facebook.com/TeenzOnTopOfficial\>
\<Instagram: teentopofficial\>
\<YouTube: www.youtube.com/TeenzOnTop\>
\<Fan Club Name: "Angel"\>

Stage Name: 캡 C.A.P
Full Name: 방민수 (Bang Min Soo)
Birth Date: 1992.11.04
Birth Place: Seoul, South Korea
Role: Leader, Main Rapper
Height: 178cm / 61kg
Bloodtype: O
Zodiac Sign: Scorpio
Chinese Zodiac Sign: Monkey
Instagram: bangminsu1992
Twitter: teentopbang
Facebook Fan Page: www.facebook.com/
C.A.PofTeenTop

―――――――――――――

Stage Name: 니엘 Niel
Full Name: 안다니엘 (Ahn Daniel)
Birth Date: 1994.08.16
Birth Place: Taean, South Korea
Role: Main Vocalist,Visual
Height: 178cm / 54kg
Bloodtype: A
Zodiac Sign: Leo
Chinese Zodiac Sign: Dog
Facebook Fan Page: www.facebook.com/
Niel-Teen-Top-212447292159081

―――――――――――――

Stage Name: 리키 Ricky
Full Name: 유창현 (Yoo Chang Hyun)
Birth Date: 1995.02.27
Birth Place: Seoul, South Korea
Role: Lead Dancer, Vocalist
Height: 172cm / 55kg
Bloodtype: AB
Zodiac Sign: Pisces
Chinese Zodiac Sign: Pig
Instagram: RICKY_TEENTOP_
Twitter: T_Ricky_T
Facebook Fan Page: www.facebook.com/
Ricky.TeenTop

―――――――――――――

Stage Name: 엘조 L.Joe
Full Name: 이병헌 (Lee Byung Hun)
Birth Date: 1993.11.22
Birth Place: Gunsan, South Korea
Role: Lead Rapper, Vocalist, Visual
Height: 171cm / 54kg
Bloodtype: A
Zodiac Sign: Sagittarius
Chinese Zodiac Sign: Rooster
Instagram: ljoeljoe931123
Twitter: ljoeljoe1123
Facebook Fan Page: www.facebook.com/
ljoeoppaoppa

―――――――――――――

\<Teen Top 틴탑\>

Stage Name: 창조 Changjo
Full Name: 최종현 (Choi Jong Hyun)
Birth Date: 1995.11.16
Birth Place: Chuncheon, South Korea
Role: Main Dancer, Vocalist, Maknae
Height: 179cm / 58kg
Bloodtype: B
Zodiac Sign: Scorpio
Chinese Zodiac Sign: Pig
Instagram: cjongh
Twitter: whdgus1004
Facebook Fan Page: www.facebook.com/
ChangJO961116

Stage Name: 천지 Chunji
Full Name: 이찬희 (Lee Chan Hee)
Birth Date: 1993.10.05
Birth Place: Seongnam, South Korea
Role: Lead Vocalist, Visual
Height: 173cm / 58kg
Zodiac Sign: Libra
Chinese Zodiac Sign: Rooster
Instagram: TEENTOP_2CH
Twitter: wowous
Facebook Fan Page: www.facebook.com/
Chunji05

★WORKS★

2013: No. 1

Singles
2010: Come into the World
2011: Transform
2012: Be Ma Girl Summer Special
2014: Snow Kiss

★FILMOGRAPHY★

DVD
2010: Making the Artist, Season 1 (GOM TV),

Road to Japan (Mnet)
2011: Making the Artist, Season 2
2012: Secret Island (Mnet), Teen Top Rising
100% (SBS MTV), Teen Top & 100% Rising
Brothers (MBC Music), Weekly Idol E. 31,
32, 49 (MBC every1)
2013: Weekly Idol Ep. 91, 115 (MBC every1)
2014: Teen Top Never Stop in Guam (Y
Star), Teen Top in Hawaii (YouTube), Weekly
Idol Ep. 167, 205 (MBC every1) 2015: Hello
Counselor Ep. 240 (KBS World)
2015: Global Request Show - A Song for You
4 Ep. 1 (KBS)

★TOURS/CONCERTS★

2012: Teen Top Japan 1st Concert Tour
2013: Teen Top 1st European Tour "Teen Top
Show!"
2013: Teen Top 1st Asia Tour Concert
2013: Teen Top Summer Special Concert
2013: Teen Top Zepp Tour "Fly Hight!")
2014: Teen Top 1st World Tour "High Kick"
2014: Teen Top Live Tour "My Dear Angels"
2015: Teen Top 5th Anniversary Concert
2016: Teen Top US Live Tour "Red Point"

★AWARDS★

2010: Rookie of the Month (Ministry of
Culture and Korea Contents Association
Awards), Power Rookie (SBS Inkigayo
Awards), Best Rookie Group (MTV Music
Awards)
2011: Rookie of the Year, New Generation of
Artists (18th Republic of Korea Entertain-
ment Arts Awards)
2013: Single Album of the Year (Golden
Disk Awards), Best Male Group (MTV Music
Awards), Idol Growth No. 2 (OBS Idol Stars
Awards), Best Music Video - "Supa Luv"

(Mnet M! Countdown Awards)
2015: Top of the Korean IDOL (Honored) (KBS
World TV)

"Roman"
2011.07.26
<TOP Media>

<Twice 트와이스>

<Meaning: "The Group Will Touch People's Hearts Twice, Once Through The Ears And Once Again Through The Eyes">
<Debut: 2015> <Company: JYP Entertainment>
<Official Page: http://twice.jype.com/> <Weibo: weibo.com/n/BaiduTWICEbar>
<V Live: www.vlive.tv/channels/EDBF> <Twitter: jypetwice>
<Facebook: www.facebook.com/JYPETWICE>
<Instagram: twicetagram>
<YouTube:http://tinyurl.com/TWICEYOUTUBE>
<Fan Club Name: "ONCE">

Stage Name: 지효 Jihyo
Full Name: 박지수 (Park Ji Soo)
Birth Date: 1997.02.01
Birth Place: Guri, South Korea
Role: Leader, Main Vocalist
Height: 162cm
Bloodtype: O
Zodiac Sign: Aquarius
Chinese Zodiac Sign: Rat
Facebook Fan Page: www.facebook.com/
TWICEJihyo

Stage Name: 나연 Nayeon
Full Name: 임나연 (Im Na Yeon)
Birth Date: 1995.09.22
Birth Place: Seoul, South Korea
Role: Lead Vocalist
Height: 163cm
Bloodtype: A
Zodiac Sign: Virgo
Chinese Zodiac Sign: Pig
Facebook Fan Page: www.facebook.com/
NayeonGoddess

Stage Name: 정연 Jungyeon
Full Name: 윤정연 (Yoo Jeong Yeon)
Birth Date: 1996.11.01
Birth Place: Suwon, South Korea
Role: Lead Vocalist
Height: 169cm
Bloodtype: O
Zodiac Sign: Scorpio
Chinese Zodiac Sign: Rat
Facebook Fan Page: www.facebook.com/
eongyeoninternational

Stage Name: 모모 Momo
Full Name: Hirai Momo
Birth Date: 1996.11.09
Birth Place: Kyoto, Japan
Role: Main Dancer, Sub Vocalist
Height: 167cm
Bloodtype: A
Zodiac Sign: Scorpio
Chinese Zodiac Sign: Rat
Facebook Fan Page: www.facebook.com/
Twice-MOMO-1009495612394797

＜Twice 트와이스＞

Stage Name: 사나 Sana
Full Name: Minatozaki Sana
Birth Date: 1996.12.29
Birth Place: Osaka, Japan
Role: Vocalist, Lead Dancer
Height: 168cm
Bloodtype: B
Zodiac Sign: Capricorn
Chinese Zodiac Sign: Rat
Facebook Fan Page: www.facebook.com/
welovesanaminatozaki

Stage Name: 미나 Mina
Full Name: Myoui Mina
Birth Date: 1997.03.24
Birth Place: Texas, United States
Role: Lead Rapper, Vocalist, Visual
Height: 163cm
Bloodtype: A
Zodiac Sign: Aries
Chinese Zodiac Sign: Ox
Facebook Fan Page: www.facebook.com/
Mina-TWICE-139323646101133

Stage Name: 다현 Dahyun
Full Name: 김다현 (Kim Da Hyun)
Birth Date: 1998.05.28
Birth Place: Seongnam, South Korea
Role: Lead Rapper, Vocalist
Height: 165cm
Bloodtype: O
Zodiac Sign: Gemini
Chinese Zodiac Sign: Tiger
Facebook Fan Page: www.facebook.com/
TWICEDahyun

Stage Name: 채영 Chaeyoung
Full Name: 손채영 (Son Chae Young)
Birth Date: 1999.04.23
Birth Place: Seoul, South Korea

Role: Main Rapper, Vocalist
Height: 163cm
Bloodtype: B
Zodiac Sign: Taurus
Chinese Zodiac Sign: Rabbit
Facebook Fan Page: www.facebook.com/
SonChaeYoung2304

Stage Name: 쯔위 Tzuyu
Full Name: Zhou Zi Yu
Birth Date: 1999.06.14
Birth Place: Tainan, Taiwan
Role: Sub Vocalist, Visual, Maknae
Height: 169cm
Bloodtype: A
Zodiac Sign: Gemini
Chinese Zodiac Sign: Rabbit
Facebook Fan Page: www.facebook.com/
TwicetzuyuJYP

★WORKS★

2015: The Story Begins
2016: Page Two
2016: TWICEcoaster : LANE 1

Singles
2015: Like Ooh-Ahh
2016: Cheer Up, TT

★FILMOGRAPHY★

Sixteen (TV series) (Mnet)
Twice TV, TV2, TV3, TV4 (V Live)
Twice's Private Life (Naver TV Cast)
Beautiful Twice (V Live)
Twice TV School Meal Club's Great Adventure (V Live)
Cheerful Twice (V Live)
Twice TV Melody Project (V Live)

<Twice 트와이스>

★TOURS/CONCERTS★
2017: Twice 1st Tour: Twiceland The Opening
South Korea (February 17-19)
Thailand (April 8)

★AWARDS★
2015: Best New Female Artist (Mnet Asian
Music Awards)
2106: Best Artist Award (Female Singer
Category) (Asia Artist Awards), Song of the
Year - "Cheer Up", Top 10 Artists (MelOn Music
Awards), Weekly Popularity Award - "Cheer Up", "TT" (MelOn Popularity Award), New Artist Award, Digital Daesang, Digital Bonsang - "Cheer Up" (Golden Disk Awards), Record of the Year in Digital Release, Bonsang Award - "Cheer Up" (Seoul Music Awards) 2017: Female Dance Performance Award - "TT" (Seoul Music Awards)

TWICE

PAGE TWO   02

"PAGE TWO" 2016.04.25
<JYP Entertainment>

‹U-KISS 유키스›

‹Meaning: "Ubiquitous Korean International Idol Super Star"›
‹Debut: 2008› ‹Company: NH Media›
‹Official Page: nhemg.com/?page_id=2193/›
‹V Live: www.vlive.tv/channels/F46159› ‹Twitter: ukisskorea›
‹Facebook: www.facebook.com/ukiss›
‹Instagram: ukisskorea_official›
‹YouTube:http://tinyurl.com/ukiss2008›
‹Fan Club Name: "Kiss Me"›

Stage Name: 수현 Soohyun
Full Name: 신수현 (Shin Soo Hyun)
Birth Date: 1989.03.11
Birth Place: Gyeonggi-do, South Korea
Role: Main Vocalist, Leader
Height: 181cm / 69kg
Bloodtype: A
Zodiac Sign: Pisces
Chinese Zodiac Sign: Snake
Instagram: shinsoohyun89
Twitter: ukissSH
Facebook Fan Page: www.facebook.com/
UKISS.Shin.Soohyun

Stage Name: 기섭 Kiseop
Full Name: 이기섭 (Lee Ki Seop)
Birth Date: 1991.01.17
Birth Place: Seoul, South Korea
Role: Main Dancer, Sub-Vocalist, Visual
Height: 181cm / 64kg
Zodiac Sign: Capricorn
Chinese Zodiac Sign: Horse
Instagram: Ki_seop91
Twitter: KiSSeop91
Facebook Fan Page: www.facebook.com/
leekiseopukiss

Stage Name: 일라이 Eli
Full Name: 김경재 (Kim Kyung Jae)
Birth Date: 1991.03.13
Birth Place: Washington, D.C., USA
Role: Main Rapper, Vocalist
Height: 180cm / 68kg
Bloodtype: O
Zodiac Sign: Pisces
Chinese Zodiac Sign: Sheep
Instagram: eli_kim91
Twitter: u_kisseli
Facebook Fan Page: www.facebook.com/
U-Kiss-Eli-179115222112781

Stage Name: 훈 Hoon
Full Name: 여훈민 (Yeo Hoon Min)
Birth Date: 1991.08.16
Birth Place: Gyeonggi-do, South Korea
Role: Lead Vocalist
Height: 181cm / 67kg
Zodiac Sign: Leo
Chinese Zodiac Sign: Sheep
Instagram: yhm1991
Twitter: HooN91y
Facebook Fan Page: www.facebook.com/
ukisshoon91

‹U-KISS 유키스›

Stage Name: 케빈 Kevin
Full Name: 우성현 (Woo Sung Hyun)
Birth Date: 1991.11.25
Birth Place: San Francisco, USA
Role: Main Vocalist, Lead Dancer, Visual
Height: 180cm / 55kg
Bloodtype: O
Zodiac Sign: Sagittarius
Chinese Zodiac Sign: Sheep
Instagram: kevin_woo1125
Twitter: Kevinwoo91
Facebook Fan Page: www.facebook.com/
KevinUkissOfficial

Stage Name: 준 Jun
Full Name: 이준영 (Lee Jun Young)
Birth Date: 1997.01.22
Birth Place: South Korea
Role: Rapper, Vocalist, Maknae
Height: 186cm / 63kg
Zodiac Sign: Aquarius
Chinese Zodiac Sign: Rat
Instagram: ukiss_jun97
Twitter: JuN97L
Facebook Fan Page: www.facebook.com/
U-Kiss-JUN-683802178377895

★WORKS★

2010: Only One
2011: Neverland
2013: Collage

Japanese
2012: A Shared Dream
2013: Inside of Me
2014: Memories
2015: Action
2016: One Shot One Kill

★FILMOGRAPHY★

2009: All About U-KISS, You Know U-KISS
2010: Autumn Destiny (Eli & Kibum) (Thailand), Chef KISS, I Am Legend (UKISS), On Air Live (Kevin), U-KISS Vampire
2011: Real School (Dongho,Kiseop & Eli) , Royal Family (Korea) (Dongho)
2012: Holy Land (Dongho & Hoon), K-Pop Tasty Road (Eli with UKISS as guest) The Strongest K-POP Survival (cameo)
2013: Beautiful Man (Hoon), Goong (Kiseop & Hoon), Kanzume!! TV Magazine Show, Summer Snow (Kevin, Soohyun & Kiseop), U-KISSme?, When A Man Loves (Hoon), After School Club Ep. 31, 73, 139 (Arirang TV)
2014 : Mental Shooter (Eli & Kevin), Go U-KISS!, Goong (Soohyun, Kiseop, Hoon & Kevin), U-KISS no Teatarishidai
2015: Cafe-In (Kiseop), Milky Love (Kevin) (Web drama), On Air~ Night Flight (Kevin & Jun), Run To You ~Street Life~ (Soohyun & Jun), Sweet Home, Sweet Honey (Hoon)
2016: More Painful Than Sadness/Never Forget (Hoon & Jun), One and Only You (Kevin and Eli), After School Club Ep. 198,216 (Arirang TV)

★TOURS/CONCERTS★

2010: U-KISS Standing Concert
2010: U-KISS 1st Kiss Live Concert
2012: U-KISS 1st Japan Live Tour
2012: U-KISS Japan Live Tour "A Shared Dream - Special Edition"
2012: U-KISS Live In Tokyo
2013: U-KISS Latinoamérica Tour
2013: U-KISS Japan Live Tour "Inside Of Me"
2014: U-KISS 1st U.S. Tour
2014: U-KISS Japan Live Tour "Memories"

\<U-KISS 유키스\>

2014: U-KISS "Scandal" In Europe Tour
2014: U-KISS "Returns" In Tokyo
2015: U-KISS Japan Live Tour "Action"
2016: U-KISS Japan Live Tour "One Shot"

★AWARDS★

2008: Best Male Idol Group (Korean Culture Entertainment Awards), Best New Male Group (Mnet Asian Music Awards), Asian Rookie Award, Influential Asian Artist (Asia Song Festival)

2010: Most Potential Overseas Artist ([V] Chinese TOP Awards)
2011: Best Male Music Video (SBS MTV Best of the Best), Photogenic Artist of the Year (Korean Video Daejun Awards)
2013: Best Male Group (Korean Culture Entertainment Awards)

"Always"
2015.01.23
\<NH Media\>

<Winner 위너>

<Meaning: "Aspire To Become The Best K-POP Band">
<Debut: 2014> <Company: YG Entertainment>
<Official Page: www.yg-winner.co.kr>
<Official Weibo: winnerasia>
<V Live: www.vlive.tv/channels/FDC2D> <Twitter: YG_WINNER>
<Facebook: www.facebook.com/OfficialYGWINNER>
<Instagram: winnercity>
<YouTube:http://tinyurl.com/OfficialYGWINNER>
<Fan Club Name: "INNERCIRCLE" (innercircle.yg-winner.com)>

Stage Name: 승윤 Seungyoon
Full Name: 강승윤 (Kang Seung Yoon)
Birth Date: 1994.01.21
Birth Place: Busan, South Korea
Role: Leader, Lead Vocalist, Maknae
Height: 178cm / 59kg
Bloodtype: B
Zodiac Sign: Aquarius
Chinese Zodiac Sign: Rooster
Instagram: w_n_r00
Facebook Fan Page: www.facebook.com/
OfficialSeungyoonKang

Stage Name: 승훈 Seunghoon
Full Name: 이승훈 (Lee Seung Hoon)
Birth Date: 1992.01.11
Birth Place: Busan, South Korea
Role: Lead Rapper, Main Dancer, Lyrics
Height: 182cm / 60kg
Bloodtype: A
Zodiac Sign: Capricorn
Chinese Zodiac Sign: Sheep
Instagram: maetamong
Facebook Fan Page: www.facebook.com/
SeungHoon.Intl

Stage Name: 민호 Mino
Full Name: 송민호 (Song Min Ho)
Birth Date: 1993.03.30
Birth Place: Yongin, South Korea
Role: Main Rapper
Height: 180cm / 67kg
Bloodtype: A
Zodiac Sign: Aries
Chinese Zodiac Sign: Rooster
Instagram: realllllmino
Facebook Fan Page: www.facebook.com/
SongMinho

Stage Name: 진우 Jinwoo
Full Name: 김진우 (Kim Jin Woo)
Birth Date: 1991.09.26
Birth Place: Imjado, South Korea
Role: Rapper, Vocalist, Visual
Height: 177cm / 54kg
Bloodtype: A
Zodiac Sign: Libra
Chinese Zodiac Sign: Rooster
Instagram: xxjjjwww
Facebook Fan Page: www.facebook.com/
OfficialJinwoo

\<Winner 위너\>

★WORKS★

2014: 2014 S/S
2014: 2014 S/S: Japan Collection
2016: EXIT:E

Singles
2013: Just Another Boy, Go Up
2014: Empty, Color Ring
2016: Pricked, Baby Baby, Sentimental

★FILMOGRAPHY★

2013: WIN: Who is Next, Winner TV (Mnet)
2014: Yoo Hee-Yeol's Sketchbook Ep. 243 (KBS2), Weekly Idol Ep. 169 (MBC every1)
2015: Yoo Hee-Yeol's Sketchbook Ep. 307 (KBS 2), Happy Camp (Human), Half-Moon Friends (JTBC)

★TOURS/CONCERTS★

2014: Winner 2014 Zepp Tour in Japan
2015: Worldwide Inner Circle Conference:
2015: Winner Japan Tour 2015
2016: Winner 2016 EXIT Tour
2016: Winner EXIT Tour in Japan 2016

★AWARDS★

2014: New Icons (Style Icon Awards), Best New Artist (Melon Music Awards), Best New Artist (Mnet Asian Music Awards), Men of the Year: New Rising (A-Awards by AREANA Homme+), Best New Artist (SBS Gayo Daejeon)
2015: New Artist of the Year (Male Group) (Gaon Chart K-Pop Awards), Best New Force Group (QQ Music Awards)
2016: Awesome K-Style (Style Icon Awards), Overseas Popularity Award (MTV Asia Music Gala)

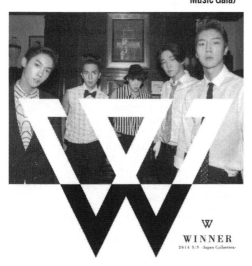

"2014 S/S Japan Collection"
2014.09.10
\< YG Entertainment\>

\<ZE:A>
\<제국의 아이들>

\<Meaning: "Children of Empire">
\<Debut: 2010> \<Company: Star Empire Entertainment>
\<Fan Cafe (Korean): cafe.daum.net/Starempire>
\<Weibo: zea20100115>
\<V Live: www.vlive.tv/channels/FB47D> \<Twitter: zea_9>
\<Facebook: www.facebook.com/ZEA2012>
\<YouTube:http://tinyurl.com/zea2011>
\<Fan Club Name: "ZE:A' STYLE">

Stage Name: 이후 Lee Hoo
Full Name: 문준영 (Moon Joon Young)
Birth Date: 1989.02.09
Birth Place: Seoul, South Korea
Role: Leader, Main Vocalist
Height: 180cm / 64kg
Bloodtype: A
Zodiac Sign: Aquarius
Chinese Zodiac Sign: Snake
Instagram: zeajunyoung
Twitter: ZEA_leader
Weibo: 5426073490
Facebook Fan Page: www.facebook.com/
MoonJunyoungOfficialFanpage

Stage Name: 시완 Siwan
Full Name: 임시완 (Lim Si Wan)
Birth Date: 1988.12.01
Birth Place: Busan, South Korea
Role: Sub Vocalist, Visual
Height: 175cm / 55kg
Bloodtype: B
Zodiac Sign: Sagittarius
Chinese Zodiac Sign: Dragon
Twitter: Siwan_ZEA
Weibo: 5453875828
Facebook Fan Page: www.facebook.com/
Siwan.ZEA

Stage Name: 케빈 Kevin
Full Name: 김지엽 (Kim Ji Yeob)
Birth Date: 1988.02.23
Birth Place: Sydney, Australia
Role: Main Vocalist
Height: 180cm / 63kg
Bloodtype: A
Zodiac Sign: Pisces
Chinese Zodiac Sign: Dragon
Instagram: kevinkim88
Facebook Fan Page: www.facebook.com/
ZEAKevin

Stage Name: 광희 Kwanghee
Full Name: 황광희 (Hwang Kwang Hee)
Birth Date: 1988.08.25
Birth Place: Paju, South Korea
Role: Sub Vocalist
Height: 175cm / 60kg
Bloodtype: A
Zodiac Sign: Virgo
Chinese Zodiac Sign: Dragon
Instagram: prince_kwanghee
Twitter: hwangkwanghee
Weibo: princekwanghee
Facebook Fan Page: www.facebook.com/
ZEAKwanghee

<ZE:A>
<제국의 아이들>

Stage Name: 태헌 Taeheon
Full Name: 김태헌 (Kim Tae Heon)
Birth Date: 1989.06.18
Birth Place: Busan, South Korea
Role: Leader, Lead Vocalist, Maknae
Height: 177cm / 63kg
Bloodtype: A
Zodiac Sign: Gemini
Chinese Zodiac Sign: Snake
Instagram: ze_a_th
Twitter: zea_th
Weibo: 5549356386
Facebook Fan Page: www.facebook.com/
ZEATaehun

Stage Name: 희철 Heechul
Full Name: 정희철 (Jung Hee Chul)
Birth Date: 1989.12.09
Birth Place: Jeju Island, South Korea
Role: Lead Rapper
Height: 177cm / 58kg
Bloodtype: B
Zodiac Sign: Sagittarius
Chinese Zodiac Sign: Snake
Instagram: heecheol1209
Weibo: 5549743931
Facebook Fan Page: www.facebook.com/
HeechulZEA

Stage Name: 민우 Minwoo
Full Name: 하민우 (Ha Min Woo)
Birth Date: 1990.09.06
Birth Place: Yangsan, South Korea
Role: Sub Vocalist, Sub Rapper, Main Dancer
Height: 178cm / 58kg
Bloodtype: B
Zodiac Sign: Virgo
Chinese Zodiac Sign: Horse
Instagram: minwoo1482
Weibo: 5548654611

Facebook Fan Page: tinyurl.com/
minwooFBFANPAGE

Stage Name: 형식 Hyungsik
Full Name: 박형식 (Park Hyung Sik)
Birth Date: 1991.11.16
Birth Place: Yongin, South Korea
Role: Main Vocalist
Height: 183cm / 64kg
Bloodtype: AB
Zodiac Sign: Virgo
Chinese Zodiac Sign: Horse
Instagram: phs1116
Twitter: zea_hyungsik
Weibo: 5487442871
Facebook Fan Page: www.facebook.com/
ZEAHyungsik

Stage Name: 동준 Dongjun
Full Name: 김동준 (Kim Dong Jun)
Birth Date: 1992.02.11
Birth Place: Busan, South Korea
Role: Lead Vocalist
Height: 175cm / 58kg
Bloodtype: B
Zodiac Sign: Aquarius
Chinese Zodiac Sign: Monkey
Instagram: super_d.j
Weibo: 5559358914
Facebook Fan Page: www.facebook.com/
ZEA.DONGJUN

★ UNIT BREAKDOWN ★
ZE:A Five (Siwan, Hyungsik, Kevin, Minwoo
& Dongjun)
ZE:A 4U (Kwanghee, Lee Hoo, Taeheon &
Heechul)
ZE:A J (Kevin, Taeheon, Heechul, Minwoo &
Dongjun)

\<ZE:A\>
\<제국의 아이들\>

★WORKS★
2011: Lovability
2012: Spectacular

Single Albums
2010: Nativity, Leap for Detonation
2011: Exiciting
2012: Phoenix

Singles
2010: Mazeltov, All Day Long, Level Up (Bad-Talk-Sad)
2011: Here I Am, Watch Out
2012: Aftereffect, Phoenix, Beautiful Lady
2013: The Ghost of the Wind
2014: Breathe

Japanese
2010: Love Letter
2011: Here I Am, Watch Out, Daily Daily

★FILMOGRAPHY★
2009: Office Reality - Children of Empire, Children of Empire Returns (Mnet)

★TOURS/CONCERTS★
2011: ZE:A Party Concert
2013: ZE:A First Concert in Korea

★AWARDS★
2010: Asia Star Award (Korea Beauty Design Awards)
2011: Top Prize (Idol Music) (Korean Art & Entertainment Awards), Minister of Ministry of Culture, Sports and Tourism Prize (Korean Popular Culture and Art Awards)

"CONTINUE"
2015.09.18
‹Star Empire Entertainment›

K★POP

QUIZ

BOOK

Over 150+ Fun-Filled Questions About Your Favorite
Idols

Q1:	Q2:
Difficulty	Difficulty
★ ★	★ ★ ★ ★
Points	Points
<5>	<10>

In 2008, this group hosted MBC's IDOL SHOW that had a total of 17 episodes.

This member of BIG BANG won the Rookie of the Year award at the 2011 Paeksang Arts Awards.

1. BtoB
2. Shinhwa
3. G.O.D.
4. 2PM
5. Big Bang

1. G-Dragon
2. T.O.P
3. Taeyang
4. Daesung
5. Seungri

Q3:
Difficulty
★ ★ ★ ★ ★
Points
<15>

This group won Malaysia's Most Favorite Award in 2013.

1. TVXQ
2. Super Junior
3. CNBLUE
4. Big Bang
5. EXO

Q4:
Difficulty
★
Points
<2>

The song "Nobody" was sung by…?

1. Wonder Girls
2. 2NE1
3. Sistar
4. AOA
5. Trouble Maker

Q5:
Difficulty
★ ★ ★ ★
Points
<10>

Q6:
Difficulty
★ ★ ★
Points
<8>

This member of AFTER SCHOOL is a licensed beautician and also has a membership at the Makeup Artist Association.

Which of the following is (was) not a member of T-ARA N4?

1. Uee
2. Nana
3. Kahi
4. Lizzy
5. Raina

1. Eunjung
2. Hyomin
3. Jiyeon
4. Choa
5. Dani

Q7:
Difficulty
★★
Points
<5>

Q8:
Difficulty
★
Points
<2>

How many members are there in SUPER JUNIOR?

BTS literally means "Bulletproof Soldiers"

1. Five
2. Nine
3. Eleven
4. Twelve
5. Fifteen

1. TRUE
2. FALSE

Q9:
Difficulty
★ ★ ★
Points
<8>

Q10:
Difficulty
★ ★ ★ ★ ★
Points
<15>

Which of the following is NOT a member of AOA BLACK?

In 2011, over 40,000 teams participated in a dance contest for THIS SONG hosted by YouTube.

1. Choa
2. Jimin
3. Yuna
4. Hara
5. Mina

1. Up and Down
2. I am the Best
3. Bar Bar Bar
4. Beep Beep
5. Rush

Q11:	Q12:
Difficulty	Difficulty
★ ★ ★	★ ★ ★ ★ ★
Points	Points
<8>	<15>

The name of TEEN TOP's official fan club is…?

Before debut, this member of BTS already had several tracks released as an underground artist, including a collaboration with ZICO.

1. Angel
2. Devil
3. Lucifer
4. Super Nova
5. Star King

1. Jin
2. Suga
3. J-Hope
4. Rap Monster
5. V

Q13:	Q14:
Difficulty	Difficulty
★ ★ ★ ★	★ ★ ★ ★
Points	Points
<10>	<10>

In 2012, Billboard named this song by INFINITE the number one KPOP song of the year.

This member was only a trainee for 3 months before JYP decided to add him to 2AM.

1. The Chaser
2. Be Mine
3. Come Back Again
4. Can U Smile
5. Bad

1. Changmin
2. Jo Kwon
3. Jay Park
4. Seulong
5. Jinwoon

Q15:
Difficulty
★ ★ ★ ★
Points
<10>

Q16:
Difficulty
★ ★ ★ ★
Points
<10>

With this title, CNBLUE won the triple crown.

Which female singer featured in 2PM's MV "10 out of 10" as a leading actress?

1. Intuition
2. Love Girl
3. I am a Loner
4. High Fly
5. Re-maintenance

1. Hyorin
2. Hara
3. Uee
4. G.Na
5. Mina

Q17:
Difficulty
★ ★
Points
<5>

BIG BANG was formed by which entertainment company?

1. SM
2. YG
3. CUBE
4. CJ
5. WOOLIM

Q18:
Difficulty
★ ★ ★ ★
Points
<10>

This group had signed ten CF contracts totaling earnings of KRW1.8 billion, which is the most for any rookie girl group after a month since debut.

1. Nine Muses
2. AOA
3. Twice
4. Wonder Girls
5. 2NE1

Q19:
Difficulty
★ ★ ★
Points
<8>

Q20:
Difficulty
★ ★
Points
<5>

Which member of
RED VELVET hosted
Music Core?

True or False:
In AOA, only
SEOLHYUN has a
male sibling.

1. Irene
2. Seulgi
3. Wendy
4. Yeri
5. Joy

1. TRUE
2. FALSE

Q21:
Difficulty
★ ★ ★ ★
Points
<10>

Q22:
Difficulty
★
Points
<2>

Son Na-eun (AOA)'s
Christian name is…?

True or False:
Kyuhyun is the
maknae of
SUPER JUNIOR.

1. Marcella
2. Maria
3. Stephanie
4. Gloria
5. Daniel

1. TRUE
2. FALSE

Which girl group sang "Ah-Choo?"

True or False: "F.T. Island" stands for "Fantastic Team Island"

1. Crayon Pop
2. Lovelyz
3. Brave Girls
4. AOA Black
5. AOA

1. TRUE
2. FALSE

Q25:
Difficulty
★ ★
Points
<5>

True or False: The lyrics of APINK's song "NANANA" secretly follows Ga-Na-Da-Ra-Ma-Ba-Sa-Ah, which is the order of letters in Hangul, Korean alphabets.

1. TRUE
2. FALSE

Q26:
Difficulty
★ ★ ★ ★ ★
Points
<15>

Twitter launched its first ever K-Pop Twitter emoji featuring…?

1. JYJ
2. CNBLUE
3. MBLAQ
4. BTS
5. Big Bang

Q27:
Difficulty
★
Points
<2>

Which of the following is not considered a TOP 3 entertainment company?

1. SM
2. JYP
3. YG
4. Show Box

Q28:
Difficulty
★
Points
<2>

Which member of 2NE1 left the group in 2016?

1. Bom
2. Dara
3. Minzy
4. CL

Q29:
Difficulty
★★★★★
Points
<15>

This group won the Best World Performer award in the 2015 Mnet Asian Music Awards.

1. BtoB
2. Shinhwa
3. G.O.D.
4. BTS
5. Big Bang

Q30:
Difficulty
★★
Points
<5>

BtoB stands for…?

1. Baby to Baby
2. Born to Beat
3. Beat to Beat
4. Boy to Boy
5. Born to Break

Q31:
Difficulty
★★
Points
<5>

4MINUTE was the first group by which entertainment company…?

1. CJ E&M
2. YG
3. JYP
4. CUBE
5. Smile Good

Q32:
Difficulty
★★
Points
<5>

ZE:A is also known as…?

1. Children of Empire
2. Zealous A-Team
3. Sweet Seven
4. Zzang Asians
5. Fantastic Baby

Q33:
Difficulty
★ ★ ★
Points
<8>

Q34:
Difficulty
★ ★
Points
<5>

The name of SISTAR's sub-unit is…?

"Cube Girls" was among the names considered for 4MINUTE

1. Sistar Four
2. Sistar19
3. Sistar Max
4. Sistar Slim
5. Sistar Project

1. TRUE
2. FALSE

Q35:
Difficulty
★ ★ ★
Points
<8>

Cho Sin Sung is the Korean name for which group?

1. Super Nova
2. Big Bang
3. T-Ara
4. SNSD
5. f(x)

Q36:
Difficulty
★ ★ ★
Points
<8>

JYJ is a subunit of which group?

1. TVXQ
2. Super Junior
3. Block B
4. Big Bang
5. EXO

Q37:
Difficulty
★ ★ ★ ★
Points
<10>

Q38:
Difficulty
★ ★ ★ ★
Points
<10>

Which member of
4MINUTE used
to be a member of
ORANGE?

This member of
APINK has the
nickname
"Tireless Energizer"

1. Hyuna
2. Sohyun
3. Soyou
4. Jiyoon
5. Gayoon

1. Yoon Bo-mi
2. Kim Nam-joo
3. Jung Eun-ji
4. Park Cho-rong
5. Oh Ha-young

Q39:
Difficulty
★ ★ ★ ★ ★
Points
<15>

Q40:
Difficulty
★ ★ ★
Points
<8>

According to the Oricon of Japan, this group has the most number-one singles for a foreign artist.

Which group appeared in the JTBC sitcom "I Live in Cheongdam-dong" as an aspiring boy band working towards their debut?

1. TVXQ
2. EXO
3. Infinite
4. Kara
5. SNSD

1. BtoB
2. Block B
3. MBLAQ
4. BTS
5. Big Bang

This member of GIRL'S DAY appeared in Answer Me 1988.

The name of Crayon Pop's first single was…?

1. Hyeri
2. 2. Sojin
3. 3. Yura
4. Minah

1. Thursday Night
2. Friday Night
3. Saturday Night
4. Sunday Night
5. Disco Night

Q43:
Difficulty
★★
Points
<5>

Q44:
Difficulty
★★★
Points
<8>

True or False: EXID stands for "Exceed in Dreaming".

Yoon Bo-mi of APINK threw the first ball at a Korean Baseball League match, and her pitch made a straight line to the catcher, which is extremely difficult for non-athletes.

1. TRUE
2. FALSE

1. TRUE
2. FALSE

Q45:
Difficulty
★★★★
Points
<10>

Q46:
Difficulty
★
Points
<2>

Before debut, T-ARA was known as…?

True or False: The members of AKDONG MUSICIAN are a married couple.

1. Super Rookies
2. Fantastic Five
3. Awesome Girls 4. Comic Girls
5. Team Ladies

1. TRUE
2. FALSE

Q47:
Difficulty
★ ★ ★
Points
<8>

Q48:
Difficulty
★ ★ ★ ★ ★
Points
<15>

INFINITE's HOYA started his acting career in…?

This group was the first non-Japanese to perform at Nissan Stadium in Japan.

1. We Got Married
2. Answer Me 1997
3. Mask
4. That Winter the Wind Blows
5. School 2015

1. 4Minute
2. EXO
3. Infinite
4. TVXQ
5. SNSD

Q49:
Difficulty
★ ★
Points
<5>

Q50:
Difficulty
★ ★ ★ ★
Points
<10>

4MINUTE debuted
with the single
titled…

"SG" of "SG
Wannabe" stands
for…?

1. Come Back
   Home
2. Don't Go
3. Hot Issue
4. I Am the Best
5. Gee

1. Simpson and
   Garfield
2. Simon and
   Garfunkel
3. Sam and George
4. Say Goodbye
5. Smile Good

This member of APINK has a third degree black belt in Taekwondo.

This member of MAMAMOO acted as the lead in the web drama "Start Love" with SS501's Kim Kyu Jong.

1. Yoon Bo-mi
. Kim Nam-joo
3. Jung Eun-ji
4. Park Cho-rong
5. Oh Ha-young

1. Solar
2. Moonbyul
3. Wheein
4. Hwasa

Q53:
Difficulty

★ ★

Points

<5>

GOT7 has members from the following countries except:

1. U.S.A
2. Korea
3. Japan
4. Hong Kong
5. Thailand

Q54:
Difficulty

★

Points

<2>

"Kkap Kwon" refers to which singer…?

1. Jay Park
2. T.O.P
3. Tae Kwon
4. Jo Kwon
5. Kwon Kim

Q55:
Difficulty
★ ★ ★
Points
<8>

Q56:
Difficulty
★ ★
Points
<5>

ORANGE CARAMEL is the first unit group of…?

True or False: YUGYEOM is the maknae of GOT7

1. Teen Top
2. AA
3. B1A4
4. Brave Girls
5. After School

1. TRUE
2. FALSE

Q57: Difficulty ★ Points <2>	Q58: Difficulty ★ ★ Points <5>
Which one of the following is a song by 2NE1?	True or False: "I.O.I" stands for "Idol of Internet"

1. I Got a Boy
2. I Don't Care
3. Liar
4. Catch Me
5. Sorry Sorry

1. TRUE
2. FALSE

Q59:	Q60:
Difficulty	Difficulty
★ ★ ★ ★ ★	★ ★ ★
Points	Points
<15>	<8>

In 2011 with their Japanese debut-single, "TAKE OFF", this group became the first Korean band to top the USEN's J-Pop Chart.

True or False: 2AM was originally modeled after 1TYM, a four-men hip hop group.

1. BtoB
2. Shinhwa
3. G.O.D.
4. 2PM
5. Big Bang

1. TRUE
2. FALSE

Q61:
Difficulty
★ ★
Points
\<5\>

Q62:
Difficulty
★ ★ ★
Points
\<8\>

True or False: "Sista" was among the many names YG considered for 2NE1

This member of APINK has been practicing Hapkido for 8 years.

1. TRUE
2. FALSE

1. Yoon Bo-mi
2. Kim Nam-joo
3. Jung Eun-ji
4. Park Cho-rong
5. Oh Ha-young

Q63:
Difficulty
★ ★ ★
Points
<8>

Q64:
Difficulty
★ ★ ★
Points
<8>

The name of MAMAMOO's debut title is?

The name of SISTAR's official debut song was…?

1. Mr. Mr.
2. Mr. Taxi
3. Mr. Ambiguous
4. Mr. Romance
5. Mr. Bad

1. Shady Girl
2. Push Push
3. Ma Boy
4. Loving U
5. Hold on Tight

Q65:
Difficulty
★ ★ ★
Points
<8>

KARA's debut title was…?

Q66:
Difficulty
★ ★ ★ ★
Points
<10>

This member of EXID participated in the pilot episode of MBC's singing competition program "King of Mask Singer". She became the first winner of the show.

1. Lupin
2. Jet Coaster Love
3. Break It
4. Step 5. Cupid

1. Hani 2. Solji
3. LE 4. Hyelin
5. Junghwa

Q67:
Difficulty
★★★★
Points
<10>

Which girl group was a part of the 2015 Feel Korea in New Delhi tour in India, performing at New Delhi's Sirifort Auditorium?

1. Baby Vox
2. S.E.S
3. Sugar
4. Bestie
5. Wonder Girls

Q68:
Difficulty
★
Points
<2>

Which girl group sang "Bar Bar Bar"?

1. Miss A
2. Twice
3. Crayon Pop
4. Sistar
5. EXID

Q69:
Difficulty
★★★★
Points
<10>

Q70:
Difficulty
★★★
Points
<8>

This group performed at an event in Mongolia, sponsored by the South Korean Embassy, with Crayon Pop and K-Much.

This member of BTS was part of a street dance team named NEURON, and was extremely active in the underground dancing scene.

1. 2NE1
2. 4Minute
3. SNSD
4. Mamamoo
5. Miss A

1. Jin
2. Suga
3. J-Hope
4. Rap Monster
5. V

Q71:
Difficulty
★★
Points
<5>

On January 16, Mnet released a preview for INFINITE's new reality show titled…

1. It's Raining
2. One Great Step
3. This is INFINITE
4. Triple Crown
5. Come Back Again

Q72:
Difficulty
★★★
Points
<8>

True or False: BLOCK B has 9 members total.

1. TRUE
2. FALSE

Q73:
Difficulty
★ ★ ★
Points
<8>

Q74:
Difficulty
★ ★ ★
Points
<8>

The name of
AOA BLACK's debut
single album is…?

APINK's EUNJI
started her acting
career in…?

1. Moya
2. Apa
3. Gajima
4. Joa
5. Hwaiting

1. Answer me 1994
2. Answer me 1997
3. The Winter the
Wind Blows
4. We Got Married
5. Mask

Q75:
Difficulty
★★
Points
<5>

Q76:
Difficulty
★★★★★
Points
<15>

Which one of the following is NOT a member of SISTAR?

This group won the MTV Iggy's "Best New Band in the World 2011" award.

1. Bora
2. Dasom
3. Soyou
4. Seohyun
5. Hyorin

1. Wonder Girls
2. 2NE1
3. Sistar
4. AOA
5. Trouble Maker

Q77:
Difficulty
★ ★
Points
<5>

True or False: JO KWON's hair is naturally curly.

Q78:
Difficulty
★ ★ ★ ★
Points
<10>

In 2010, this group was invited to perform in Japan's "Hallyu Music Festival". They were the only Korean girl group.

1. TRUE
2. FALSE

1. SNSD
2. Sistar19
3. AOA
4. Sistar
5. Miss A

CHOA of AOA played this character in HIGH SCHOOL MUSICAL.

Which of the following is NOT a member of AFTERSCHOOL?

1. Kelsi
2. Gabriella
3. Ashley
4. Leslie
5. Monique

1. Uee
2. Raina
3. Nana
4. Hara
5. Lizzy

Q81:
Difficulty
★ ★ ★
Points
<8>

Miss A's SUZY debuted as an actress in…?

1. Dream High
2. Architecture 101
3. Uncontrollably Fond
4. Dorihwaga 5. Winter Sonata

Q82:
Difficulty
★ ★ ★
Points
<8>

ZE:A has how many members?

1. Three
2. Five
3. Seven
4. Nine
5. Eleven

Q83:
Difficulty
★ ★ ★ ★
Points
<10>

Before debuting, this member of I.O.I appeared on the web drama "To Be Continued".

1. Lim Na-young 2. Choi Yoo-jung
3. Kim Chung-ha 4. Zhou Jieqiong
5. Kim Do-yeon

Q84:
Difficulty
★ ★ ★
Points
<8>

FIESTAR was a 6-member team until who left the group?

1. Cheska
2. Jei
3. Cao Lu
4. Linzy
5. Hyemi

Q85:
Difficulty
★ ★ ★
Points
<8>

Q86:
Difficulty
★ ★
Points
<5>

Which member of RED VELVET hosted Music Bank?

True or False: All of the members of B1A4 are from the country side, so often the Korean media call them "COUNTRYSIDE DOLS"

1. Irene
2. Seulgi
3. Wendy
4. Yeri
5. Joy

1. TRUE
2. FALSE

Q87:
Difficulty
★★
Points
<5>

Q88:
Difficulty
★★★
Points
<8>

True or False: 2NE1 stands for ""21st Century" and "New Evolution".

Which member of AOA won first place in 2010 Smart uniform model contest.

1. TRUE
2. FALSE

1. Seolhyun
2. Hyejeong
3. Chanmi
4. Choa
5. Mina

Q89:
Difficulty
★ ★
Points
<5>

Q90:
Difficulty
★ ★ ★
Points
<8>

Which member of EXID formed a sub-unit DASONI with Hani?

DARA's brother is this member from MBLAQ.

1. LE
2. Hyerin
3. Solji
4. Junghwa

1. Seungho
2. Mir
3. Thunder
4. G.O
5. Lee Joon

TWICE has a member who is originally from Taiwan. Who is she?

This member of 2NE1 is trilingual - Korean, English, and French.

1. Dahyun
2. Tzuyu
3. Mina
4. Nayeon
5. Jihyo

1. Bom
2. Dara
3. Minzy
4. CL

This member of MAMAMOO appeared in King of Mask Singer, disguised as a sunflower.

This member of ZE:A formed a unit group with two Japanese artists, called 3Peace Lovers.

1. Solar
2. Moonbyul
3. Wheein
4. Hwasa

1. Kevin
2. Siwan
3. Minwoo
4. Lee Hoo
5. Heechul

Q95:
Difficulty
★ ★ ★ ★
Points
<10>

Before their official debut, MAMAMOO collaborated with BUMKEY and released this song.

1. Don't Be Happy
2. Peppermint Chocolate
3. Ah Oop
4. Um Oh Ah Yeh 5. I Miss You

Q96:
Difficulty
★ ★
Points
<5>

Which member of TWICE is from Osaka, Japan?

1. Momo
2. Sana
3. Mina
4. Jihyo
5. Nayeon

True or False: JUNGHWA is the maknae of EXID

True or False: B1A4 was first introduced through a webtoon.

1. TRUE
2. 2. FALSE

1. TRUE
2. FALSE

Q99:
Difficulty
★★
Points
<5>

Q100:
Difficulty
★★★
Points
<8>

The name of AOA's fan club is…?

The name of CNBLUE's fan club is…?

1. El Dorado
2. AOA of Elvis
3. El Angelitas
4. Ace of Aces
5. Eternity

1. Boice
2. Black Rain
3. Blue Black
4. Blue Rain
5. Blue Ribbon

| Q101:
Difficulty
★ ★
Points
<5> | Q102:
Difficulty
★
Points
<2> |

MISS A stands for…?　NICHKHUN of 2PM is from…?

1. Miss Adorable	1. China
2. Miss Asia	2. Russia
3. Miss Aegyo	3. France
4. Miss April	4. Thailand
5. Miss Artistic	5. North Korea

True or False: 2AM is a ballad group.

Who is the leader of CNBLUE?

1. TRUE
2. FALSE

1. Lee Jong-hyun
2. Kang Min-hyuk
3. Lee Jung-shin
4. Jung Yong-hwa

Following CNBLUE, this group was the 2nd K-Pop group to perform in Australia.

RED VELVET was formed by which entertainment company?

1. 4Minute
2. 2NE1
3. Big Bang
4. 2PM
5. 2AM

1. SM
2. YG
3. CUBE
4. CJ
5. WOOLIM

Q111:
Difficulty
★★
Points
<5>

Q112:
Difficulty
★★★
Points
<8>

"Do You Wanna B?" was the name of this group's debut title…

How many members are there in SHINEE?

1. TVXQ
2. Super Junior
3. Block B
4. Big Bang
5. EXO

1. Two
2. Three
3. Four
4. Five
5. Six

Q113:
Difficulty
★ ★ ★ ★
Points
<10>

Q114:
Difficulty
★ ★
Points
<5>

Block B was created by which famous Korean rapper…?

True or False: B.E.G stands for "Black Eyed Girls"

1. Zion T
2. Dynamic Duo
3. Outsider
4. Cho PD
5. YDG

1. TRUE 2. FALSE

True or False: CNBLUE debuted their first mini-album in Korea with the lead single "I'm a Loner".

GAYOON and JIYOON made a mini unit called 2YOON, and their music genre was…?

1. Country Pop
2. Hip Hop
3. EDM
4. Trot
5. Ballad

1. TRUE
2. FALSE

Which boy group sang the song "Beep Beep?

Which member of CNBLUE took his film role in the Chinese-language "Emperors Cook Up a Storm"?

1. Block B
2. 2PM
3. 2AM
4. Big Bang
5. BtoB

1. Lee Jong-hyun
2. Kang Min-hyuk
3. Lee Jung-shin
4. Jung Yong-hwa

Q119:

Difficulty

★ ★ ★ ★

Points

<10>

Which of the following was the girl dancing crew in BEAST/B2ST's song "BEAUTIFUL".

1. APINK
2. AOA
3. 4Minute
4. 2NE1
5. f(x)

Q120:

Difficulty

★ ★

Points

<5>

Which of the following is NOT a member of EXO?

1. Suho
2. Lay
3. Chen
4. Chanyeol
5. Mir

This group was named by Forbes as the most retweeted artist on Twitter in March 2016.

In 2009, this group was invited to "Live in Malaysia" hosted by MTV. and was the only group that performed at the after party.

1. BtoB
2. Block B
3. MBLAQ
4. BTS
5. Big Bang

1. 2AM
2. Big Bang
3. Teen Top
4. Super Junior
5. AOA

Q123:
Difficulty
★★★★★
Points
<15>

Q124:
Difficulty
★★★★★
Points
<15>

This member of TWICE was originally set to debut in a group called 6mix.

This group was the first Korean Idol group to be invited to perform at Times Square in New York.

1. Momo
2. Jeongyeon
3. Mina
4. Jihyo
5. Nayeon

1. 2NE1
2. AOA
3. 4Minute
4. Miss A
5. EXID

AOA stands for…?

True or False: "SS" of "SS501" stands for "Superstar Singer"

1. Ace of Angels
2. Apple Orange Apricot
3. After Our Anniversary
4. Anything of Anything
5. Always Anytime

1. TRUE 2. FALSE

Q127:
Difficulty
★ ★ ★
Points
<8>

Q128:
Difficulty
★ ★ ★
Points
<8>

True or False: TVXQ stands for "Rising Gods of the East"

True or False: BTS was the first KPOP group to open a VEVO account.

1. TRUE
2. FALSE

1. TRUE
2. FALSE

Q129:
Difficulty
★ ★ ★
Points
<8>

Q130:
Difficulty
★ ★ ★
Points
<8>

Which member is the maknae of BEAST?

Which member of B1A4 won an Ulzzang contest?

1. Dongwon
2. Gikwang
3. Yoseob
4. Junhyung
5. Doojoon

1. Baro
2. Jinyoung
3. Gongchan
4. G-Dragon
5. Taeyang

Q131:	Q132:
Difficulty	Difficulty
★★★	★
Points	Points
<8>	<2>

INFINITE's first album was titled…?

Jay Park used to be a member of which group…?

1. Over the Top
2. Fly to the Sky
3. Come Back Again
4. Evolution
5. Revolution

1. 2AM
2. 2PM
3. Big Bang
4. SNSD
5. G.O.D

Q133:
Difficulty
★★
Points
<5>

Q134:
Difficulty
★★
Points
<5>

True or False: JUN. K's original name was KIM JUN-SOO which later he changed to KIM MIN-JUN, after his father passed away.

True or False: 2AM hosted a comedy show "Gag Concert".

1. TRUE 2. FALSE

1. TRUE 2. FALSE

Q135:
Difficulty
★★★★★
Points
<15>

Q136:
Difficulty
★★
Points
<5>

This song was used as the background music for Microsoft's Surface Pro 3 TV commercial in the U.S.

True or False: APINK's members are all rappers. There are no designated vocalists.

1. Up and Down
2. I am the Best
3. Bar Bar Bar
4. Beep Beep
5. Rush

1. TRUE 2. FALSE

Q137:
Difficulty
★
Points
<2>

Q138:
Difficulty
★★
Points
<5>

TROUBLE MAKER
is a duo formed by
Jang Hyun-seung and
who?

True or False: YG
discovered DARA
while watching
MBC's "Infinity
Challenge"

1. Tzuyu 2. Mina
3. Hyuna 4. Bora
5. Taeyeon

1. TRUE
2. FALSE

"GROUP OF NATURAL DISASTERS" is another nickname for this group, because there were numerous natural disasters that coincided with their concert schedule.

True or False: STELLAR was originally produced by Kim Dongwan of Shinhwa.

1. AOA
2. 4Minute
3. 2NE1
4. Miss A 5. EXID

1. TRUE
2. FALSE

True or False:
SPICA's debut album
was titled "Russian
Roulette".

This group was
labeled as "K-pop's
Social Conscience"
by Jeff Benjamin from
Fuse.

1. TRUE
2. FALSE

1. BTS
2. 2NE1
3. BtoB
4. Super Junior
5. Miss A

Before joining 2NE1, this member was an actress in the Philippines.

MBLAQ is a band created by…?

1. CL
2. Minzy
3. Bom
4. Dara

1. JYP 2. Rain
3. G-Dragon
4. T.O.P
5. Eric Nam

Q145:
Difficulty
★★★★
Points
<10>

Which group was revealed to have ranked as the most powerful celebrity by Forbes Korea for the year 2015?

1. TVXQ
2. Super Junior
3. Block B
4. Big Bang
5. EXO

Q146:
Difficulty
★★★
Points
<8>

Which member of BEAST left the group in 2016?

1. Hyunseung
2. Dongwon
3. Gikwang
4. Yoseob
5. Junhyung

Q147:
Difficulty
★ ★ ★ ★
Points
<10>

This group had the opening act for Lady Gaga's ArtRave: The Artpop Ball concert tour in twelve cities across North America.

1. Crayon Pop
2. Wonder Girls
3. Sistar 4. AOA
5. After School

Q148:
Difficulty
★ ★ ★
Points
<8>

This member of ZE:A received national fame for his role in the MBC's fictional historical drama "The Moon That Embraces The Sun" playing the teen version of the prince's scholar, Heo Yeom.

1. Kevin 2. Siwan
3. Kwanghee
4. Lee Hoo
5. Heechul

Q149:
Difficulty
★ ★ ★
Points
<8>

Q150:
Difficulty
★ ★
Points
<5>

In 2010, this group appeared in the Mnet reality show "You Are My Oppa."

Which member of ZE:A is a member of MBC's Infinity(Infinite) Challenge TV show?

1. Infinite
2. CNBLUE
3. 2AM
4. 2PM
5. MBLAQ

1. Kevin
2. Siwan
3. Kwanghee
4. Lee Hoo
5. Heechul

Q151:
Difficulty
★★★
Points
<8>

Q152:
Difficulty
★★
Points
<5>

True or False: In the 'street version' of 2NE1's music video "FIRE", TAEYANG appears as a cameo.

"Black Jack" is the name of this group's fan club.

1. TRUE
2. FALSE

1. Brave Girls
2. 2NE1
3. Twice
4. Miss A
5. EXID

Q153:
Difficulty
★ ★ ★
Points
<8>

Q154:
Difficulty
★ ★ ★
Points
<8>

True or False: None of the members of APINK, is blood type A

Which member of RED VELVET was in the TV show "We Got Married"?

1. TRUE
2. FALSE

1. Irene
2. Seulgi
3. Wendy
4. Yeri
5. Joy

The first KPOP group to perform at SXSW?

The song "10 out of 10" was sung by…?

1. f(x)
2. CNBLUE
3. Red Velvet
4. Big Bang
5. Teen Top

1. Super Junior
2. Crayon Pop
3. 2PM
4. ZE:A
5. EXO

Q157:
Difficulty
★ ★ ★
Points
<8>

Before their official
debut, this group
made the first
appearance through a
TV commercial which
co-featured Big Bang.

1. Wonder Girls
2. 2NE1
3. Sistar
4. AOA
5. Trouble Maker

ANSWER KEYS

1.	2PM
2.	T.O.P
3.	CNBLUE
4.	Wonder Girls
5.	Nana
6.	Choa
7.	Eleven
8.	FALSE (Bullet Proof Boy Scouts)
9.	Hara
10.	I am the Best
11.	Angel
12.	Rap Monster
13.	The Chaser
14.	Changmin
15.	Intuition
16.	G.Na
17.	YG
18.	Twice
19.	Yeri
20.	FALSE (None of the members have a male sibling.)
21.	Marcella
22.	TRUE
23.	Lovelyz
24.	FALSE (Five Treasure Island)
25.	TRUE
26.	BTS
27.	Show Box
28.	Minzy
29.	BTS
30.	Born to Beat
31.	CUBE
32.	Children of Empire
33.	Sistar19
34.	TRUE
35.	Super Nova
36.	TVXQ
37.	Sohyun
38.	Kim Nam-joo
39.	TVXQ
40.	BtoB
41.	Hyeri
42.	Saturday Night
43.	TRUE
44.	TRUE
45.	Super Rookies
46.	FALSE (They are siblings)
47.	Answer Me 1997
48.	TVXQ
49.	Hot Issue
50.	Simon and Garfunkel
51.	Yoon Bo-mi
52.	Moonbyul
53.	Japan
54.	Jo Kwon
55.	After School
56.	TRUE
57.	I Don't Care
58.	FALSE (Ideal of Idol)
59.	2PM

60. FALSE (They were originally modeled after NOEL)
61. TRUE
62. Park Cho-rong
63. Mr. Ambiguous
64. Push Push
65. Break It
66. Solji
67. Bestie
68. Crayon Pop
69. Mamamoo
70. J-Hope
71. This is INFINITE
72. FALSE (Seven)
73. Moya
74. Answer me 1997
75. Seohyun
76. 2NE1
77. Sistar
78. Sistar
79. Gabriella
80. Hara
81. Dream High
82. Nine
83. Choi Yoo-jung
84. Cheska
85. Irene
86. TRUE
87. TRUE
88. Seolhyun
89. Solji
90. Thunder
91. Tzuyu
92. CL
93. Solar
94. Minwoo
95. Don't Be Happy
96. Sana
97. TRUE
98. TRUE
99. AOA of Elvis
100. Boice
101. Miss Asia
102. Thailand
103. TRUE
104. Jung Yong-hwa
105. 4Minute
106. SM
107. Wonder Girls
108. Pearl Black
109. CNBLUE
110. Eight
111. Block B
112. Five
113. Cho PD
114. FALSE (Brown Eyed Girls)
115. TRUE
116. Country Pop
117. BtoB
118. Jung Yong-hwa
119. APINK
120. Mir
121. BTS
122. 2AM

123. Jeongyeon
124. 2NE1
125. Ace of Angels
126. TRUE
127. TRUE
128. FALSE (4Minute)
129. Dongwon
130. Gongchan
131. Over the Top
132. 2PM
133. TRUE
134. FALSE (2AM hosted a comedy show SNL Korea, Season 4, Episode 8.)
135. I am the Best
136. FALSE (APINK's members are all vocalists. There are no designated rappers.)
137. Hyuna
138. FALSE (YG discovered DARA while watching a KBS documentary "MY NAME IS SANDARA PARK".)
139. 2NE1
140. FALSE (Eric Mun)
141. TRUE
142. BTS
143. Dara
144. Rain
145. EXO
146. Hyunseung
147. Crayon Pop
148. Siwan
149. Infinite
150. Kwanghee
151. FALSE (G-Dragon)
152. 2NE1
153. TRUE
154. Joy
155. f(x)
156. 2PM
157. 2NE1

How To Write A Kpop Fan Mail / Letter In Korean

Why write a fan mail?

► You have a crush on a KPOP idol.
► You are so deeply moved by their work and want them to know that.
► Your life has changed so much (for the better) and you want to express your gratitude.
► You want them to know that you exist.
► You want them to know that there are people like you who love and care for them.
► You think about them 24/7 and just can't get them out of your head.

But whatever the reason is, KPOP idols feed off their fans' love and support. Think about it — whenever they win an award, they always express their gratitude to their fans. They exist because of you. So not only is it to make you feel better, it is actually one of the best ways to keep them motivated and energized. It is something they need the most when they are down, because in reality, they are just like us. Sending them a fan mail full of love and support is like giving them a hug.

Word of advice

▶ Be polite. They are human beings who deserve respect just like you.

▶ Don't be too polite or too formal. They want a friend and a supporter who can feel comfortable hanging out with.

▶ Don't be a creepy stalker. This doesn't need to be explained.

▶ Don't expect a reply. They get hundreds of fan letters every day.

▶ But don't assume they all go straight to the trash. They, or someone close to them (e.g., their manager or staff members will take the time to read them).

▶ Don't be afraid of grammatical errors. Even if your Korean is not perfect, it's the thought and effort that count. They are not your Korean language teachers. Even if you make some errors, they can still feel what you are trying to say.

▶ Do decorate your letters, if you want to.

▶ Do keep it short and interesting.

▶ Do use neat handwriting, but bad handwriting is better than a typed letter.

▶ Do have it proofread. Best if you have a Korean friend around.

▶ Do check with your local post office to make sure how many stamps to put on the envelope.

How to compose your letter

►Introduce yourself

They want to know you as much as you do. Talk about your name, where your home town is, your age and other fun bits of information such as your blood type and nickname.

►Talk about why you like them so much

This is the part your idol looks forward to reading the most! Show them your love and support.

►Talk about what they mean to you

Do they give you an inspiration? Did they change your life?

►Say thank you

Express your gratitude.

►Closing remarks

Wrap up the letter and include a wish/request if you want.

Labeling the envelope

English Version Sample

Korean Version Sample

While both English and Korean versions are acceptable, We'd recommend the Korean version as the Korean post office employees/ mail carriers will find it easier to understand. Make sure, however, that you write SEOUL, SOUTH KOREA in English, so that your country's post office knows where it's going.

*앞 means To/Attn. Add it to the receiver's name (e.g., 씨엘 (CL) 앞)
**우) means postal code (short for 우편번호).

Where to send them

JYP Entertainment

(2PM, Wonder Girls, 2AM, miss A, Baek A Yeon, 15&,
SUNMI, GOT7, Bernard Park, G.Soul, DAY6, TWICE, SUZY,
SOMI)

JYP Entertainment
41 Apgujeong-ro 79-gil, Cheongdam-dong,
Gangnam-gu, SEOUL 06012
SOUTH KOREA
Attn: (Your Idol's Name)

서울시 강남구 압구정로 79길 41
JYP 센터
(Your Idol's Name) 앞
우) 06012
SEOUL, SOUTH KOREA

Plan A Entertainment

(Apink, Huh Gak, Jung Eun-ji)

Plan A Entertainment
Star Hill Building 6F, 151, Bongeunsa-ro,
Gangnam-gu, SEOUL 06122
SOUTH KOREA
Attn: (Your Idol's Name)

서울 강남구 봉은사로 151 스타힐빌딩 6층
플랜에이엔터테인먼트
(Your Idol's Name) 앞
우) 06122
SEOUL, SOUTH KOREA

FNC Entertainment

(AOA, CN Blue, FT Island, SF9, N.Fying, Jung Yong Hwa,
Lee Hong Gi, JIMIN, INNOVATOR)

FNC Entertainment
46 Dosan-daero 85-gil, Cheongdam-dong,
Gangnam-gu, SEOUL 06012
SOUTH KOREA
Attn: (Your Idol's Name)

서울특별시 강남구 도산대로85길 46
FNC 엔터테인먼트
(Your Idol's Name) 앞
우) 06012
SEOUL, SOUTH KOREA

Fantagio Music

(Astro)

Fantagio Music
248, Yeoksam-ro,
Gangnam-gu, SEOUL 06226
SOUTH KOREA
Attn: (Your Idol's Name)

서울특별시 강남구 역삼로 248
판타지오
(Your Idol's Name) 앞
우) 06226
SEOUL, SOUTH KOREA

Big Hit Entertainment
(BTS)

Big Hit Entertainment
Cheonggu Building 2F
13-20, Dosan-daero 16-gil
Gangnam-gu, Seoul 06040
SOUTH KOREA
Attn: (Your Idol's Name)

서울특별시 강남구 도산대로16길 13-20
청구빌딩 2층
빅히트 엔터테인먼트
(Your Idol's Name) 앞
우) 06040
SEOUL, SOUTH KOREA

YG Entertainment
(Big Bang, Black Pink, Psy, Mobb, 2NE1, Winner, iKON, SechsKies, Epik High, Akdong Musician, Lee Hi, CL)

YG Entertainment
397-5 Hapjeong-dong,
Mapo-gu, SEOUL 04028
SOUTH KOREA
Attn: (Your Idol's Name)

서울특별시 마포구 합정동 397-5
YG 엔터테인먼트
(Your Idol's Name) 앞
우) 04028
SEOUL, SOUTH KOREA

TS Entertainment

(BAP, Secret, Untouchable, Sonamoo, Sleepy, D.Action,
Song Ji Eun, Jun Hyo Seong, Bang & Zelo, Bang Yong Guk)

TS Entertainment
31, Hannam-daero 40-gil,
Yongsan-gu, SEOUL 04417
SOUTH KOREA
Attn: (Your Idol's Name)

서울특별시 용산구 한남대로40길 31
TS 엔터테인먼트
(Your Idol's Name) 앞
우) 04417
SEOUL, SOUTH KOREA

WM Entertainment

(B1A4, Oh My Girl, (I), Sandeul)

WM Entertainment
8, World Cup-ro 15-gil,
Mapo-gu, SEOUL 04012
SOUTH KOREA
Attn: (Your Idol's Name)

서울특별시 마포구 월드컵로15길 8
WM 엔터테인먼트
(Your Idol's Name) 앞
우) 04012
SEOUL, SOUTH KOREA

Around Us Entertainment
(BEAST)

Around Us Entertainment
37-1, Apgujeong-ro 79-gil,
Gangnam-gu, SEOUL 06012
SOUTH KOREA
Attn: (Your Idol's Name)

서울특별시 강남구 청담동 123-45
어라운드 어스 엔터테인먼트
(Your Idol's Name) 앞
우) 06012
SEOUL, SOUTH KOREA

Banana Culture Entertainment
(EXID)

Banana Culture Entertainment
5, Seongsuil-ro 8-gil, Seongdong-gu
Mapo-gu SEOUL 04793
SOUTH KOREA
Attn: (Your Idol's Name)

서울특별시 성동구 성수일로8길 5
서울숲 SK V1타워 B동 지하 1층
바나나컬쳐 엔터테인먼트
(Your Idol's Name) 앞
우) 04793
SEOUL, SOUTH KOREA

KQ Entertainment
(Block B)

KQ Entertainment
Jay Studio 3F
28, Donggyo-ro 25-gil,
Mapo-gu, SEOUL 03993
SOUTH KOREA
Attn: (Your Idol's Name)

서울특별시 마포구 동교로 25길 28,
제이스튜디오 3층
KQ 엔터테인먼트
(Your Idol's Name) 앞
우) 03993
SEOUL, SOUTH KOREA

Cube Entertainment
(BtoB, Hyuna, Jang Hyun Seung, CLC, Trouble Maker, Roh
Jihoon, Pentagon, Kim Kiri, Na Jongchan)

Cube Entertainment
F2 Building
83 Achasan-ro,
Seongdong-gu, Seoul SEOUL 04793
SOUTH KOREA
Attn: (Your Idol's Name)

서울특별시 성동구 아차산로 83
F2빌딩
큐브 엔터테인먼트
(Your Idol's Name) 앞
우) 04793
SEOUL, SOUTH KOREA

SM Entertainment

(EXO, TBXQ, TRAX, Super Junior, Girls' Generation, SHINee, f(x), Red Velvet, NCT, BoA, ZhangLiYin)

SM Entertainment
648, Samseong-ro, Gangnam-gu
Gangnam-gu, SEOUL 06084
SOUTH KOREA
Attn: (Your Idol's Name)

서울특별시 강남구 삼성로 648
SM 엔터테인먼트
(Your Idol's Name) 앞
우) 06084
SEOUL, SOUTH KOREA

Woollim Entertainment

(Jang Jun & Young Taek, Joo Chan & So Yoon, INFINITE)

Woollim Entertainment
14, World Cup buk-ro 23-gil,
Mapo-gu, SEOUL 03966
SOUTH KOREA
Attn: (Your Idol's Name)

서울특별시 마포구 월드컵북로 23길 14
울림 엔터테인먼트
(Your Idol's Name) 앞
우) 03966
SEOUL, SOUTH KOREA

RBW Entertainment

(MAMAMOO, VROMANCE, Basick, Yangpa, Monday Kiz, O
Broject, eSNa, Big Tray)

RBW Entertainment
7, Janghan-Ro, 20-Gil,
Dongdaemun-Gu, SEOUL 02639
SOUTH KOREA
Attn: (Your Idol's Name)

서울특별시 동대문구 장한로20길 7
RBW 엔터테인먼트
(Your Idol's Name) 앞
우) 02639
SEOUL, SOUTH KOREA

NH MEDIA

(Lim Chang Jung, U-KISS, LABOUM, The Ray,
SOUL LATIDO)

NH MEDIA
10-23 Nonhyeon 1-dong,
Mapo-gu, SEOUL 06040
SOUTH KOREA
Attn: (Your Idol's Name)

서울특별시 강남구 논현1동 10-23
NH 미디어
(Your Idol's Name) 앞
우) 06040
SEOUL, SOUTH KOREA

TOP MEDIA

(ANDY, TEENTOP, 100%, PARK Dong Min, UP10TION)

TOP Media
47, Bongeunsa-ro 55-gil,
Gangnam-gu, SEOUL 06093
SOUTH KOREA
Attn: (Your Idol's Name)

서울특별시 강남구 봉은사로55길 47
티오피 미디어
(Your Idol's Name) 앞
우) 06093
SEOUL, SOUTH KOREA

Starship Entertainment

(K.WILL, Sistar, Boyfriend, Mad Clown, Jung Gi Go,
MONSTA X, BrotherSu, WJSN, #GUN)

Starship Entertainment
Starhill Building 4F
151, Bongeunsa-ro,
Gangnam-gu, SEOUL 06122
SOUTH KOREA
Attn: (Your Idol's Name)

서울특별시 강남구 봉은사로 151
스타빌딩 4층
스타쉽엔터테인먼트
(Your Idol's Name) 앞
우) 06122
SEOUL, SOUTH KOREA

Star Empire Entertainment

(Nine Muses, ZE:A, Seo In Young, Impact)

Star Empire Entertainment
48, Seongji-gil,
Mapo-gu, SEOUL 04083
SOUTH KOREA
Attn: (Your Idol's Name)

서울특별시 마포구 성지길 48
스타제국
(Your Idol's Name) 앞
우) 04083
SEOUL, SOUTH KOREA

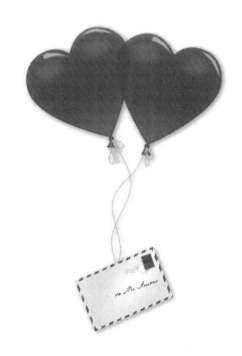

Fan Mail
Expressions

How to Use The Expressions

The expressions are customizable, meaning that you can create your own sentence by inserting the words you want. Those fields are presented in parenthesis so you know exactly what goes where. Simply pick, customize, and combine the expressions of your choice and you just wrote a KPOP fan letter in Korean that sounds 100% natural!

Some useful tips:

► How to address your idol

Some of the most commonly used ones are:

〉 오빠 – If you are a younger female addressing an older male idol.
Example) GD 오빠, 안녕하세요?

〉 형 – If you are a younger male addressing an older male idol.
Example) Tony 형, 안녕하세요?

〉 누나 – If you are a younger male addressing an older female idol.
Example)
BoA 누나, 만나서 반가워요!

〉 언니 - If you are a younger female addressing an older female idol.
Example) Jenny 언니, 정말 예뻐요!

〉 당신 - If you want to address someone you don't know in a formal way. It is used on its own.

Example) 당신은 정말 멋있어요!

〉 ~씨 - If you want to address someone you don't know in a formal way using the name.

Example) GD씨, 안녕하세요?

〉 ~야 - If you want to be extra friendly. It is used between friends of same age, to someone younger.

Example) Tony야, 안녕?

► How to choose the proper direct object particle "을/를"

〉 If your word ends with a vowel (ㅏ / ㅑ / ㅓ / ㅕ / ㅗ / ㅛ / ㅜ / ㅠ / ㅡ / ㅣ / ㅒ / ㅖ / ㅘ / ㅙ / ㅝ / ㅞ / ㅚ / ㅟ / ㅢ), use "를"

Example) 소미 (Somi) 를, 오빠 (oppa) 를, 나 (na) 를

〉 If your word ends with a consonant, use "을"

*It's not the English spelling that matters. The rule applies to how the Korean word ends. For example, while 컴퓨터 (computer) is spelled to end with a consonant in English, the Korean word ends with a vowel " ㅓ ". Hence you use "를"

Example) 빅뱅 (Big Bang) 을, 지드래곤 (G-Dragon) 을, SM 타운 (SM Town) 을

▶ How to choose the proper topic particle "는/은"

〉 If your word ends with a vowel, use "는"
Example) 바나나 (banana) 는, 오빠 (oppa) 는, 블랙핑크 (Black Pink) 는

*Again, while Black Pink ends with a consonant in English, it ends with a vowel
"ㅡ" in Korean. Hence you use "는"

〉 If your words ends with a consonant, use "은"

Example) 빅뱅 (Big Bang) 은, 지드래곤 (G-Dragon) 은, 레드벨벳 (Red Velvet) 은.

▶ How to choose the proper subject particle "이/가"

〉 If your word ends with a vowel, use "가"
Example) GD 오빠 (GD oppa) 가, 아이유 언니 (IU unnie) 가

> If your words ends with a consonant, use "이"

Example) 빅뱅 (Big Bang) 이, 레드벨벳 (Red Velvet) 이.

► **Use an online Korean dictionary to find the words you need.**

Whenever you come across a customizable blank, use any of the following to find the Korean word for it.

Google translator – translate.google.com (best for Western languages (English, Spanish, French, and etc.)

Naver translator – translate.naver.com (best for Asian languages (Chinese, Japanese, Thai, Indonesian, Vietnamese, and etc.)

Greetings & Introduction

1. (   ) 에게,
To/Dear (   ),

2. 사랑하는 (   ) 에게,
To my dearest (   ),

3. 안녕?
Hello/Hi (informal, between friends)

4. 안녕하세요?
Hello/Hi/How are you? (formal)

5. 잘 지냈어요?
How have you been?
(literal meaning : Have you been well?)

6. 어떻게 지냈어요?
How have you been?

7. 그동안 별 일 없었어요?
Anything new down your way?

8. 정말 오랜만이에요!
It really has been a long time!

9. 오랜만에 편지를 써요.
It's been a while since I wrote to you.

10. (만나서/알게되어서) 기뻐요.
It's a pleasure (meeting/knowing) you.

11. 처음으로 (   ) 에게 편지를 써요.
This is my first time writing a letter to you.

12. 제 이름은 (   ) 이에요.
My name is (   ).

13. 저는 (   ) 이에요.
I am (a) (   ).

Example) 학생 – student, 멕시코 사람 –
Mexican, 중국 사람 – Chinese, 필리핀 사람
– Filipino 프랑스 사람 – French 영국 사람 –
English (British)

14. 제 혈액형은 (   ) 이에요.
My blood type is (   ).

15. 저는 (   ) 에 살아요.
I live in (   ).

16. 한국어 잘 못해요.
My Korean isn't very good. / My Korean is poor.

17. 한국어 공부하고 있어요.
I am studying Korean.

18. 한국어 잘 못해서 미안해요.
I am sorry my Korean isn't good.

19. 한국어 잘 못하지만 이해해 주세요.
Please excuse my bad (poor) Korean.

20. 친구가 도와주고 있어요.
My friend is helping me out.

21. 친구도 (   ) 팬이에요.
My friend is also a fan of (   ).

22. 혼자서 한국어로 편지 쓰고 싶어요.
I want to write a letter in Korean by myself.

23. 한국어 잘하고 싶어요.
I want to be good at Korean.

24. 한국어 공부 열심히해서 (   ) 에게 제 마음을 전하고 싶어요.
I want to study Korean hard so I can express my feelings to (   ).

25. 한국어 공부는 정말 어려워요.
Studying Korean is very difficult.

26. 하지만 최선을 다할거에요.
But I will do my very best.

27. (   ) 에게 하고 싶은 이야기가 많아요.
I have so many things to share with you/tell you.

28. 저는 (   ) 에 살아요.
I live in (   ).

29. 저는 (   ) 살 이에요.
I am (   ) years old.

30. 제 별명은 (   ) 이에요.
People call me / My nickname is (   ).

31. 저는 (엄마/아빠/강아지) 와 함께 살아요.
I live with (mom/dad/puppy).

32. 저는 (   ) 에서 태어났어요.
I was born in (   ).

33. 저는 (   ) 출신이에요.
I am from / I come from (   ).

34. 이곳은 (   ) 마을 / 도시 에요.
It is a (   ) village / city.

35. 이곳은 (   ) 로 유명해요.
It is famous for (   ).

36. 저는 (   ) 에게 편지 쓰려고 한국어를 공부해요.
I study Korean so I can write a letter to you.

37. 저는 (   )* 를(을) (   )** 동안 좋아했어요.
I have been a fan of (   )* for (   )**. / I've loved (   )* since (   )**.

38. 한국에 가보고 싶어요.
I want to visit Korea.

39. 우리 (   ) 때 (   ) 에서 만났어요.
We've met at a (   ) in/at (   ).

40. 우리는 만난적은 없어요.
We've never met.

41. (   ) 생각만 하면 웃음이 나와요.
Just thinking about you makes me smile.

42. (   ) 는(은) 나를 웃게 만들어요.
(   ) make(s) me smile.

43. (   ) 의 노래/목소리를 들으면
눈물이 나요.
I cry when I hear/listen to (   ) song/
voice.

44. (   ) 의 노래/목소리를 들으면
에너지가 생겨요.
I become full of energy when I hear/listen to
(   ) song/voice.

45. (   ) 의 얼굴/video를 보면 눈물이
나요.
I cry when I see (   ) face/video.

46. (   ) 의 얼굴/video를 보면 에너지가
생겨요.
I become full of energy when I see (   )
face/video.

47. (   ) 가(이) 나와 같은 하늘 아래에
살고 있다는 사실에 기분이 너무좋아요.
The fact that (   ) and I live under the
same sky (in the same world) makes me feel
so happy.

48. (   ) 는(은) (   ) 를(을)
좋아해요?
Do(es) (   ) like (   )?

49. (콘서트/사인회/시사회/TV쇼/영화)**에서
(   )* 를 보았어요.
I saw (   )* at/in (concert/fan signing/
movie screening/TV show/movie)**.

50. 데뷔때부터 팬이었어요.
I've been a fan since debut.

51. 당신과 같은 사람은 이 세상에 없어요.
There is no one like you in the world.

52. (   ) 를(을) 본 순간부터 사랑에
빠졌어요.
I fell in love from the moment I saw (   ).

53. (오빠)* (목소리/노래)** 를(을) 들은
순간부터 사랑에 빠졌어요.

I fell in love from the moment I heard
(oppa=your)* (voice/song)**.

54. (   ) 는(은) 정말 (예뻐/멋있어/
잘생겼어/아름다워/사랑스러워/똑똑해/
재밌어)*요.
(   ) is/are so (pretty/cool/handsome/
beautiful/lovely/smart/funny)*.

55. (   ) 는(은) 세상에서 가장 (예뻐/
멋있어/잘생겼어/아름다워/사랑스러워/
똑똑해/재밌어)요.
(   ) is/are the prettiest/coolest/most
handsome/most beautiful/loveliest/smartest/
funniest

56. (   ) 는(은) 친절한 사람이에요.
(   ) is/are a kind person.

57. (   ) 의 건강과 행복을 위해 기도해요.
I pray for your health and happiness.

58. (   ) 가(이) 아프면 나도 아파요.
When (   ) is/are sick (hurt), I feel sick
(hurt) too.

59. (   ) 가(이) 슬프면 나도 슬퍼요.
When (   ) is/are sad, I feel sad too.

60. (   ) 가(이) 행복하면 나도 행복해요.
If (   ) is/are happy, I feel happy too.

61. (   ) 는(은) (노래/댄스/연기/공부/
기타연주/공연)* 할때 가장 (예뻐/멋있어/
잘생겼어/아름다워/사랑스러워/재밌어)**요.
(   ) is/are/look the (prettiest/coolest/
most handsome/most beautiful/loveliest/
funniest)** when (singing/dancing/acting/
studying/playing the guitar/performing)*.

62. (   ) 는(은) 저에게 큰 영감이에요.
(   ) is/are a huge inspiration to me.

63. (   ) 의 콘서트에 갈거에요.
I am going to (   ) concert.

64. (   )의 콘서트에 갔었어요.
I went to (   ) concert.

65. 매일 (   ) 의 노래를 들어요.
I listen to (   ) song everyday.

66. >매일 (   ) 가 나오는 영상을 봐요.
I watch (   ) video clips everyday.

67. (   ) 의 콘서트에 가는게 제
소원이에요.
I really wish to go to (   ) concert.

68. 항상 보고싶어요.
I always miss you.

69. 항상 (   ) 생각해요.
I always think about you.

70. 자나깨나 (   ) 생각해요.
I think about (   ) 24/7

71. 가슴이 너무 뛰어요.
My heart is pounding so fast.

72. 정말 정말 행복해요.
I am really really happy.

~ Useful Words ~

73. 최근에 (recently)

74. 마지막으로 (lastly)

75. 처음으로 (for the first time)

76. 다시 한번 (one more time)

77. 진짜로 (really)

78. 솔직히 (honestly / frankly)

79. 솔직히 말해서 (frankly speaking)

80. 진심으로 (wholeheartedly)

81. 언제나 (always)

82. 매일 (everyday)

Expressing Gratitude

83. 고마워요.
Thank you.

84. 감사합니다.
I appreciate it.

85. 언제나 훌륭한 (노래/영화/드라마/music video)에 감사하고 있어요.
I am always grateful for your outstanding (song/movie/drama/music video).

86. 팬들을 생각해줘서 고마워요.
Thank you for thinking of your fans.

87. (   )없는 세상은 상상하기 싫어요.
I don't want to imagine a world without (   ).

88. 모든 팬들이 고마워해요.
All of the fans are thankful for it.

89. (   ) 덕분에 많은것이 바뀌었어요.
Because of (   ), lots of things have changed.

90. 물론, 좋은 쪽으로요.
For the better, of course.

91. 희망을 주어서 고마워요.
Thank you for giving me a hope.

92. 여러가지로 고마워요.
Thank you for everything.

93. 덕분에 매일 행복해요.
Thanks to you, I am happy everyday.

94. 고마움으로 가득해요.
I am full of gratitude.

95. 언제나 고맙다고 말하고 싶었어요.
I've always wanted to say thank you.

96. 부끄러움을 좀 타지만, 고마워요.
I am a little shy to say this, but thank you.

97. 고맙다는 표현을 어떻게 해야 충분한지
모르겠어요.
I don't know how to thank you enough.

98. 많이 고맙다는 뜻이에요.
That means I am really thankful for it.

99. 고마움에 보답할게요.
I will repay you for your kindness.

100. (   )는(은) 정말 친절한 사람이에요.
(   ) is/are a really kind person.

101. (   )는(은) 정말 친절하고 상냥해요.
(   ) is/are really kind and friendly.

102. (   ) 덕분에 웃어요.
I smile because of (   ).

103. (   )는(은) 나의 기쁨이에요.
(   ) is/are my pleasure.

104. 세상에 와줘서 고마워요.
Thank you for coming to this world.

105. 얼마나 고마운지 몰라요!
You don't even know how thankful I am!

106. 진심으로 감사합니다.
I sincerely appreciate it.

107. 깊이 감사드리고 있어요.
I'm deeply grateful to you.

108. 어쨌든 정말 고마워요.

Thank you so much anyway.

109. 도와줘서 고마워요.
Thank you for helping me.

110. 기다려줘서 고마워요.
Thank you for waiting.

111. 걱정해줘서 고마워요.
Thank you for your concern.

112. 작지만 감사의 표시에요.
This is a small token of appreciation.

113. 우리는 매우 감사하고 고마워하고 있어요.
We are very appreciative end very grateful.

114. 다시 한번 (   )의 노고에 감사드려요.
Thank you again for (   ) hard work.

115. 시간 내주셔서 고마워요.
Thank you for your time.

116. 바쁘실텐데 제 편지 읽어주셔서 고마워요.
Thank you for taking the time out of your busy
schedule to read my letter.

117. 친절을 베풀어주셔서 깊이 감사드려요.

I thank you from the bottom of my heart for your kindness.

118. 뭐라고 감사해야 할 지 모르겠어요.
I have no words to express my gratitude.

119. 저에게 영감을 주셔서 고마워요.
Thank you for being my inspiration.

120. 저에게 큰 힘이 되어주셔서 고마워요.
Thank you for being a great encouragement.

121. 그렇게 말해주니 고마워요,
It's kind of you to say that.

122. 어떻게 보답해야 할까요?
How can I ever repay you?

123. 큰 힘이 되어주었어요.
You've been a great help.

124. (   ) 에게 고맙다고 전해주세요.
Please give my thanks to (   ).

125. 정말 행복해요.
I am really happy.

126. 행복하게 만들어줘서 고마워요.
Thank you for making me happy.

127. 매일 행복해요.
I am happy everyday.

128. 이렇게 행복했던 적은 없어요.
I've never been this happy.

129. 밥을 안먹어도 배가 불러요.
I feel full without eating = (I'm happy 24/7).

130. 행복이란 이런 느낌인가봐요.
This must be what happiness feels like.

131. 행복/사랑 이라는 것을 알게 해주었어요.
You taught me what happiness/love feels like.

132. 항상 고마워 하며 살게요.
I will always be thankful to you.

133. (   )에 와주셔서 고마워요!
Thanks for coming to (   )!

134. (   )에서 콘서트를 해주셔서
고마워요!
Thanks for having a concert in/at (   )!

135. 훌륭한 롤모델이 되어줘서 고마워요!
Thanks for being a great role model!

136. 언제나 웃음을 잃지 않아줘서 고마워요!
Thank you for always having a smile on your face!

137. 최고가 되어줘서 고마워요.
Thank you for being the best.

138. 이 세상에 단 하나뿐인 존재가 되어줘서 고마워요.
Thank you for being the one and only.

139. (저를/우리를)잊지 않아줘서 고마워요.
Thank you for not forgetting (me/us).

140. (저를/우리를) 특별하게 만들어 줘서 고마워요.
Thank you for making (me/us) feel special.

~ Useful Words ~

141. 항상 (always)
Example) 항상 보고싶어요. (I always miss you.)

142. ~에서 (at/in/on)
Example) 콘서트에서 (at a concert) 무대에서 (on the stage)

143. 이 세상에 (in this world)
144. ~에게 (to)
Example) 오빠에게 (to oppa)

145. ~덕분에 (thanks to)
Example) 오빠 덕분에 (thanks to oppa)

146. 웃어요 (I smile)

147. 행복해요 (I am happy)

Congratulatory Messages

148. 축하해요!
Congratulations!

149. 축하합니다!
Congratulations (formal).

150. 생일 축하합니다!
Happy Birthday! (literal meaning = I
congratulate your birthday)

151. (대상/본상) 타신것 축하해요!
Congratulations on winning the daesang/
bonsang!

152. 상 타실 것 알고있었어요.
I knew you'd win that award.

153. 새 앨범 나온 것 축하해요!
Congratulations on your new album release!

154. (드라마/영화/TV쇼)에 캐스팅 되신 것
축하해요!
Congratulations on getting a role in the
(drama/movie/TV show).

155. (　　　) 주년을 축하해요!
Happy (　　　) anniversary!

156. 데뷔 (　　　) 주년을 축하해요!
Happy (　　　) debut anniversary!

157. 1등을 축하해요!
Congratulations on being #!

158. 차트 1등을 축하해요!
Congratulations on topping the chart!

159. 차트 올킬을 축하해요!
Congratulations on "all-killing" the charts!

160. 트리플 크라운을 축하해요!
Congratulations on achieving "Triple Crown"!

161. 새로 나온 (뮤직비디오/노래) 정말 멋져요!
The newly released (music video/song) is really awesome!

162. 새 (헤어 스타일/패션) 정말 멋져요!
Your new (hair style/fashion) is so cool!

163. 새 앨범에 있는 곡들 전부 다 좋아요!
I like every single song in the new album.

164. 새 (컨셉/CF/안무) 정말 (멋져요/
섹시해요/신비해요).
The new (concept/CF/choreograph) is really
(cool/sexy/mysterious).

165. 진심으로 축하해요!
I extend to you my heartiest congratulations!

166. 새 멤버가 생긴걸 축하해요!
Congratulations on the new addition to the
group! (= new member to the group)

167. 그럴 자격이 있어요!
You deserve it! / You earned it!

168. 해냈어요!
You did it! / You made it!

169. 계속 잘 해주세요!
Keep up the good work!

~ Useful Words ~

170. 새 (new) + noun
Example) 새 신발 (new shoes)

171. 새로 나온 (newly released) + noun

Example) 새로 나온 영화 (newly released movie)

172. Noun + 좋아요 (I like ~sth) : Example) 강아지 좋아요 (I like puppies)

173. ~(number) 주년 (~th anniversary) : Example) 주년 (th year anniversary)

174. 생일 (birthday) / 상 (award) / 1등 (1st place)

175. 노래 (song)

Compliments

176. (　　　　) 팬들이 정말 많아요.
(　　　　) have so many fans here.

177. 팬클럽 회원이 정말 많아요.
The fan club has so many members.

178. 모두 (　　　　) 의 팬이에요.
We are all fans of (　　　　).

179. (　　　　) 은/는 춤을 정말 잘춰요.
(　　　　) is/are such a great dancer.

180. (연기/노래)를 어떻게 그렇게 잘해요?
How can you be so good at (acting/singing)?

181. 어떻게 그렇게 (예뻐요/멋져요/
잘생겼어요/웃겨요/재밌어요)?
How can you be so (pretty/cool/handsome/
hilarious/funny)?

182. 왜 그렇게 (예뻐요/멋져요/잘생겼어요/
웃겨요/재밌어요)?
Why are you so (pretty/cool/handsome/
hilarious/funny)?

183. 언제부터 그렇게 (예뻤어요/멋졌어요/
잘생겼었어요/웃겼어요/재밌었어요)?
Since when have you been so (pretty/cool/
handsome/hilarious/funny)?

184. 매력이 넘쳐요.
You are very charming.

185. 매력 덩어리에요.
You are full of charm = You are my
McDreamy.

186. 최고에요.
You are the best.

187. 최고중의 최고에요.
You are the best of the best.

188. (   )를/을 제일 좋아해요.
I like (   ) the most.

189. (   ) 는(은) 정말 특별해요.
(   ) is/are so special.

190. (   ) 는(은) 세상에 단 하나밖에 없는
사람이에요.
(   ) is/are the one and only person in
the world.

191. (   ) 는(은) 하늘이 주신 선물이에요.
(   ) is/are a gift from heaven.

192. (   ) 는(은) 내 인생에 가장 큰
선물이에요.
(   ) is/are the greatest gift/present of
my life.

193. (   ) 는(은) 내 인생의 큰 의미에요.
(   ) mean(s) a lot in my life.

194. (   ) 없는 세상은 너무 외롭고 슬플
것 같아요.
The world without (   ) will be so lonely
and sad.

195. (   ) 는(은) 천사같아요.
(   ) is/are like an angel.

196. (   ) 는(은) 나에게 모든것이에요.
(   ) mean(s) everything to me.

197. 목소리가 정말 달콤해요/섹시해요.
Your voice is so sweet/sexy.

198. 모두에게 친절해서 좋아요.
I like the fact that you are kind to everyone.

199. 똑똑하고 친절해요.
You are smart and kind.

200. 정말 완벽해요.
You are really perfect.

201. 완벽 그 자체에요.
You are perfection itself.

202. 모든걸 다 가진 사람이에요.
You are a man who has everything.

203. 저도 (   ) 처럼 되고 싶어요.
I want to be like (   ).

204. (   ) 이/가 정말 (예뻐요/멋져요/섹시해요).
Your (   ) is/are so pretty/cool/sexy.

205. 유머 감각이 뛰어나세요.
You have a great sense of humor.

206. 몸매가 정말 좋으세요.
You are in such great shape.

207. (   )를/을 닮으셨어요.
You look like (   ).

208. (   )* 를 보면 (   )**
생각이나요.
(   )* remind me of (   )**.

209. 어떻게 몸매를 유지해요?
How do you stay in shape?

210. 훌륭한 남편이 될거에요.
You will make a great husband.

211. 훌륭한 아내가 될거에요.
You will make a great wife.

212. 당당함이 멋져요.
I admire your confidence.

213. 타고난 리더에요.
You are a natural-born leader.

214. 모두들 당신을 존경해요.
Everyone looks up to you.

215. 우리 모두의 우상이에요.
You are our idol.

216. 우리는 (   )을 숭배해요!
We worship (   ).

217. (   ) 는/은 우리의 수호천사에요.
(   ) is/are our guardian angel.

218. (   ) 이/가 함께 있다고 생각하면
마음이 든든해요.
I feel safe when I think (   ) is/are with
me.

219. 존재만으로도 힘이되요.
Your mere existence is a great support.

220. (   )의 노래를 들으면 힘이 솟아요!
Listening to (   ) song gives me energy!

221. (   ) 는/은 눈부신 빛과 같아요.
(   ) is/are like a bright light.

222. (   ) 는/은 태양과 같이 밝아요.
(   ) is/are bright like the sun.

223. 내 인생의 태양.
The sun of my life.

224. 내 인생의 (의미/목적).
The meaning/purpose of my life.

225. 내가 아침에 눈을 뜨는 이유.

The reason I open my eyes in the morning.

226. 내가 살아가는 이유.
The reason I live.

227. 그게 바로 (   )입니다.
That is because of (   ).

228. 나도 (   )에게 힘이 되고 싶어요.
I also want to be your support.

~ Useful Words ~

229. 우리는 (we are)
Example) 우리는 행복해요. We are happy.

230. 나도 (I also, me too)
Example) 나도 행복해요. I am also happy.

231. 어떻게 (how)

232. 왜 (why)

233. ~같아요 (look/feel/sound like ~ sth)
Example) 강아지 같아요. You (look) like a puppy.

234. 화이팅!
Fighting (= cheer up! / let's go!)

235. 힘내요!
Cheer up!

236. 잘 될 거에요!
It's going to be all right!

237. 성공할거에요!
It will be a success!

238. 대박을 기원합니다.
Hope you win it big! (= wishing you the best of luck!)

239. 성공은 따놓은 당상이에요.
There is no doubt it will be a success.

240. 잘 했어요!
Way to go!

241. 짱이에요! (= informal 최고에요!)
You are the best!

242. 믿을 수가 없어요!
Unbelievable!

243. 생각보다 훨씬 (멋져요/예뻐요/섹시해요/잘생겼어요/좋아요)
It's cooler/prettier/sexier/more handsome/better than I've imagined.

244. 언제나 응원합니다.
I'm always on your side.

245. 언제나 응원하는거 알죠?
You know I'm always on your side, right?

246. 우리가 있잖아요!
We are here for you!

247. 걱정할 필요 없어요.
There is no need to worry.

248. 걱정마세요.
Don't worry about it.

249. 하나도 걱정하지 마세요.
Don't you worry about a thing.

250. 성공은 당연해요.
Your success is guaranteed.

251. 우리가 서포트해요.
We will be there to support.

252. (   ) 를(을) 사랑하는 팬들이 정말
많아요.
There are many fans who love (   ).

253. (저/우리)가 (   )에 응원하러
갈거에요.
I/We will be at (   ) to support you.

254. 큰 소리로 외칠거에요.
I will cry at the top of my voice.

255. 함께 노래 할거에요.
I will sing along with you.

256. 형광봉을 흔들거에요.
I will be waving a light stick.

257. 정말 환상적일거에요.
It will be really fantastic.

258. 꿈꿔왔던 순간이 될거에요.
It will be a dream-come-true moment.

259. 실수해도 괜찮아요.
It's okay if you make a mistake.

260. 어떻게 해도 사랑스러워요.
You are lovely, no matter what.

261. 행동 하나 하나가 사랑스러워요.
Every single move you make is lovely.

262. 실패해도 괜찮아요.
It's okay if you fail.

263. 다음에 더 잘할거에요.
You will do better next time.

264. 제 느낌은 틀린적이 없어요.
My feelings have never been wrong.

265. 좋은 느낌이 들어요.
I have a good feeling about it.

266. 끝내줬어요!
That was awesome! (informal = That was the bomb!)

267. 힘들땐 (제/우리) 생각을 해주세요.
Please think about me/us whenever you are feeling down.

268. 항상 기도할거에요.
I will always be praying for you.

269. 본방사수 할거에요!
I will watch it live!

270. 대상 타기를 기원할게요!
I wish you win the grand prize!

271. 반드시 1등 할거에요!
I am sure you will win the first place!

272. 울지 말아요!
Please don't cry!

273. 안타깝지만, 슬퍼하지 말아요.
It is a pity (= it is a shame), but don't feel sad.

274. 다음이 있잖아요!
There is always next time!

275. 엄청난 신인이에요!
You are an amazing rookie!

276. (   ) 의 뉴스를 보았어요.
I saw the news about (   ).

277. (   )의 이야기를 들었어요.
I heard the story about (   ).

278. 저는 언제나 (   ) 를(을) 믿어요.
I always trust (   ).

279. 그런 소문따위 믿지 않아요.
I don't believe the rumors.

280. (   )만 믿어요.
I only believe in (   ).

281. 누가 뭐라고 하던지.
No matter what they say.

282. 다른사람들이 하는 말 신경쓰지 마세요.
Don't worry about what others say.

283. 다른사람들이 하는 생각 신경쓰지 마세요.
Don't worry about what other people think.

284. 그냥 하는 일에만 집중하세요.
Just focus on what you are doing.

285. 그게 (제가/우리가) 원하는 것이에요.
That's what I/we want.

286. 제 편지를 보고 힘내세요!
I hope my letter cheers you up!

287. 좋은 생각과 기운을 보냅니다.

Sending good thoughts and vibes.

288. 저는 (   ) 가(이) 정말 자랑스러워요.
I am really proud of (   ).

289. (   ) 는(은) 제 인생을 바꾸었어요.
(   ) changed my life.

290. (   ) 덕분에 힘든 시간을 버텨낼 수
있었어요.
Thanks to (   ), I was able to persevere
through the hard times.

291. (   ) 는(은) 제 은인이에요!
(   ) is/are the savior of my life! / I am
very indebted to (   ).

~ Useful Words ~

292. 믿어요 (I believe)

293. 힘내세요! (cheer up!)

294. 하나도 (not even a thing, not at all)
Example) 하나도 안 무서워요 not afraid at all

295. 알죠? You know, right?

Expressing Concerns

296. 아프지 말아요.
Don't get sick.

297. 많이 아프다고 들었어요.
I heard you are very sick.

298. 마음이 많이 아프겠어요.
You must be heartbroken.

299. 많이 슬프겠어요.
You must be very sad.

300. 우울해하지 말아요.
Don't be so depressed.

301. 많이 다쳤어요?
Are you badly hurt?

302. 많이 다치지 않았으면 좋겠어요.
I hope you are not too hurt.

303. 많이 슬퍼하지 않았으면 좋겠어요.
I hope you don't feel too bad.

304. 빨리 나으세요.
I hope you get better soon.

305. 우리 모두 걱정하고 있어요.
We are all worried.

306. 너무 걱정되요.
I'm so worried.

307. (   )에 대해서 너무 걱정이 되요.
I am so worried about (   ).

308. 걱정하게 만들지 말아주세요.
Please don't make me worry.

309. 실망 많이 했죠?
You must have been so disappointed.

310. 많이 힘들었죠?
You must have suffered a lot.

311. 얼마나 힘들었을까.
I can't imagine how difficult it must have been.

312. 모두 다 괜찮아 질거에요.
Everything will be all right.

313. 힘들때는 좀 쉬어요.
Try to take a break when you feel exhausted.

314. 완벽한 사람은 없어요.
Nobody's perfect.

315. 물론, (　　　　　)은/는 완벽에 가장 가까운 사람이지만요.
Of course, you are the closest thing to perfection.

316. 너무 열심히 일하지 마세요.
Don't work too hard.

317. 안티는 무시하세요.
Just ignore anti fans.

318. 부러워서 그러는거에요.
They act like that because they are jealous.

319. 괜찮을 것 같아요?
You think you will be okay?

320. 괜찮을 거라고 생각해요.
I think you will be all right.

321. 울지 말아요!
Don't cry.

322. 너무 기쁠때만 울어요!
Cry only when you are too happy!

323. 어떻게 하면 (제/우리)가 도움이 될 수 있을까요?
How can I/we be of help?

324. 건강이 가장 중요해요.
Health is the most important thing.

325. 밥 잘 챙겨 먹어요.
Don't skip meals.

326. 술 너무 많이 마시지 마세요.
Don't drink too much.

327. 파티 너무 많이 하지 마세요.
Don't party too hard.

328. 몸에 좋은 것 많이 먹어요.
Eat lots of things that are good for your body.

329. 잠 많이 자요.
Sleep a lot.

330. 운전 조심해요.
Drive carefully.

331. 음주운전은 절대 안되요!
Drunk driving is never okay!

332. 문자 하면서 (운전하지/걸어가지) 말아요.
Don't text while driving/walking on the street.

333. (   )의 행복이 (저/우리)의
행복이에요!
Your happiness is my/our happiness!

334. 싸우지 말아요.
Don't fight

335. 멤버들끼리 사이좋게 지내세요.
Please get along with your members.

336. 서로 조금씩 양보해요.
Each should give in a little.

337. (제/우리) 걱정은 하지 마세요.
Don't worry about me/us.

~ Useful Words ~

338. 완벽한 (perfect)

339. 걱정 (worry)

340. 양보 (yield/to give in)

341. 안티 (anti fans)

342. 물론 (of course)

Wishes & Requests

343. (   ) 에 꼭 와주세요!
I really hope that you would visit us in (
).

344. (   ) 에 다시 와주기를 기원할게요!
I wish you to come back to visit us in (
)!

345. 하지만 꼭 만나고 싶어요.
But I really want to meet you.

346. 언젠가는 만날거라고 믿어요.
I believe we will meet sometime.

347. 언젠가는 꿈이 꼭 이루어 질거라고 믿어요.
I believe that dreams will come true one day.

348. (   ) 를(을) 만나게 되면 세상에서
가장 행복할 것 같아요.
I think I will be the happiest person in the
world if I met (   ).

349. (   ) 를(을) 만나게 되면 너무 좋아서
눈물이 날 것 같아요.

I think I will cry tears of joy if I meet (   ).

350. (   ) 의 손을 잡고 싶어요.
I want to hold (   ) hand.

351. (   ) 와 함께 걷고 싶어요.
I want to walk with (   ).

352. (   ) 와 함께 노래부르고 싶어요.
I want to sing with (   ).

353. (   ) 와 함께 영화보고 싶어요.
I want to go to the movies with (   ).

354. (   ) 와 함께 사진찍고 싶어요.
I want to take a picture with (   ).

355. (   ) 와 함께 여행하고 싶어요.
I want to travel with (   ).

356. (   ) 와 함께 데이트하고 싶어요.
I want to go on a date with (   ).

357. (   ) 와 결혼하고 싶어요.
I want to marry (   ).

358. (   ) 의 여자친구가 되고 싶어요.
I want to be (   ) girlfriend.

359. (　　　　) 의 남자친구가 되고 싶어요.
I want to be (　　　　) boyfriend.

360. (　　　　) 가(이) 항상 제 곁에 있어주었으면 좋겠어요.
I always want to have you right here by my side.

361. 실물로 만나보고 싶어요.
I want to meet you in the flesh.

362. 라이브로 보고 싶어요.
I want to see it live.

363. 팬들을 위해 열심히 해주세요!
Please do your very best for the fans!

364. 빠른 시일내에 다시 보고 싶어요.
I hope to see you again in the near future.

365. 너무 오래 기다리지 않았으면 좋겠어요.
I hope I wouldn't have to wait too long.

366. 자주 앨범 내 주세요.
Please release albums more often.

367. (뮤직비디오/노래) 더 많이 만들어주세요.
Please make more music video/songs.

368. (   )와 콜라보 해주세요!
Please do a collaborative work with (   )!

369. (TV show name) 에 나와주세요!
Please be on (TV show name)

370. 사진 보내주세요!
Please send me a photo!

371. 싸인 해주세요!
Please give me your autograph!

372. 인증샷 찍어주세요!
Please make sure to take a proof shot!

373. 운동 열심히 하세요!
Please work out hard!

374. 기도 열심히 하세요!
Please pray hard!

375. 공부 열심히 하세요!
Please study hard!

376. 답장 해주세요!
Please write me back!

377. 제 선물 마음에 들었으면 좋겠어요!

I hope you like my gift!

378. 선물을 보면 제 생각을 해 주세요.
Please think of me when you look at my gift.

379. 제 편지 간직해주세요.
Please keep my letter!

380. 저를 잊지 말아주세요.
Don't forget me.

381. (Kakao ID/Instagram/Facebook)
알려주세요.
Please tell me your .(Kakao ID/Instagram/
Facebook).

382. 제 (Kakao ID/Instagram/Facebook) 은/는
(   ) 이에요.
(   ) is my (Kakao ID/Instagram/
Facebook)

383. 친구 추가 해주세요.
Please add me as a friend.

384. 제 전화번호는 (   ) 이에요.
My phone number is (   ).

385. 전화해 주세요!
Please call me!

384. 선물 (gift)

385. 친구 (friend)

386. ~해주세요 (please do me ~sth)
Example) 노래 해주세요 (please sing me a song)

387. 편지 (letter/mail)

388. 언젠가는 (one day)

Closing statement

389. 사랑해요!
I love you! / We love you!

390. 항상 사랑해요!
I always love you! / We always love you!

391. 절대 잊지 않을게요!
I will never forget you! / We will never forget you!

392. 자주 방송에 나와주세요.
Please be on TV shows more often!

393. (TV쇼/콘서트/극장) 에서 볼게요!
I will see you at/on (TV show/concert/theater)

394. 행운을 빌어요.
Good luck to you.

395. 신의 가호가 있기를!
May the grace of God be with you!

396. 행운의 여신이 함께 하기를!
May the lady luck be with you!

397. 즐거운 여행 되세요!
Have a fun trip!

398. 다시 만날때까지.
Until we meet again.

399. 그때를 기다릴게요.
I will wait for that moment.

400. 어디에 있어도
Wherever you are

401. 언제, 어디서나
Whenever, wherever

402. 웃음을 잃지 말아요
Don't forget to smile

403. 또 편지 할게요.
I will write you again.

404. 기다려주세요!
Please wait for me!

405. 사라지지 말아요!
Don't disappear!

406. 얼굴 좀 자주 보여주세요.

Show us your face more often.

407. 항상 건강하세요.
Always be healthy.

408. 빨리 컴백하주세요!
I hope you make a comeback very soon!

409. 군대에서 돌아올때까지 기다릴게요.
I will wait until you come back from the army.

410. 시간은 금방 지나갈거에요.
Time will fly.

411. 인내심을 갖고 기다릴게요.
I will wait patiently.

412. 너무 바쁜 것 알아요.
I know you are very busy.

413. 답장 못해줘도 실망하지 않을거에요.
I won't be disappointed if you can't write me.

414. 시간 내서 편지 읽어줘서 고마워요.
Thank you for taking the time to read my letter.

415. 행복하세요!

Be happy!

416. 잘 지내요!
Take care!

417. 보고싶을 거에요.
I will miss you.

418. ( )가
From ( )

~ Useful Words ~

419. 즐거운 (pleasant / joyful / entertaining)
Example) 즐거운 노래 (joyful song)

420. 자주 (often)

421. 또 (again)

422. ~할게요 (I will~)
Example) 노래 할게요 (I will sing a song)

Fan Mail
Templates &
Samples

(태양 오빠)에게,
Dear Taeyang oppa,

안녕하세요? 제 이름은 (안드레아) 에요. 저는 (브라질)에 살아요. 저는 (12)살 이에요.
Hi, how are you? My name is (Andrea). I live in (Brazil). I am (12) years old.

처음으로 (오빠)에게 편지를 써요. 한국어 잘 못 하지만 이해해주세요. 하지만 최선을 다할거에요.
This is my first time writing a letter to (oppa=you). Please excuse my bad Korean. But I will do my best.

(오빠)의 노래를 들으면 눈물이나요. 데뷔때부터 팬이었어요. (오빠)의 (콘서트)에 갔었어요.
I cry when I hear/listen to (your) song. I've been a fan since debut. I went to (your) (concert).

(오빠)는 저에게 큰 영감이에요. 매일 (오빠)의 노래를 들어요. 정말 정말 행복해요.
(You) are a huge inspiration to me. I always listen to (your) song. I am really really happy.

언제나 훌륭한 (노래)에 감사하고 있어요. 모든

팬들이 고마워해요.
I am always grateful for your outstanding (song). All the fans are thankful for it.

또 편지 할게요. 항상 웃음을 잃지 마세요.
I will write you again soon. Please don't forget to smile.

(안드레아)가
From (Andrea)

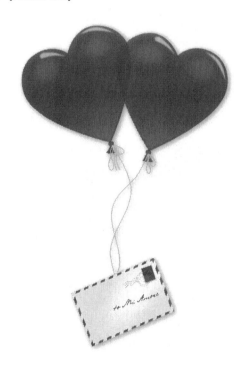

(아이유 언니)에게
Dear (IU unnie),

오랜만에 편지를 써요. 그동안 별일 없었어요?
(언니)에게 하고 싶은 이야기가 많아요.
It's been a while since I wrote to you. Anything new down your way? I have so many
things to share with (unnie=you).

(언니)의 뉴스를 보았어요. 저는 언제나 (언니)를
믿어요. 누가 뭐라고 하던지. 그런 소문따위 믿
지 않아요.
I saw the news about (you). I always trust
(you). Whatevery they say. I don't believe the
rumors.

많이 슬프겠어요. 안티는 무시하세요. 부러워서
그러는거에요.
You must be very sad. Just ignore anti fans.
They act like that because they are jealous.

건강이 가장 중요해요. (언니)의 행복이 (저)의
행복잉요.
Health is the most important thing. (Your)
happiness is (my) happiness.

(제)걱정은 하지 말아요.
Don't worry about (me).

또 편지 할게요.
I will write you again.

(지니)가
From (Jinny)

(앰버 씨)에게
Dear (Amber (formal)),

안녕하세요? 제 이름은 (마이클)이에요. (알게되어서) 기뻐요.
Hi, how are you? My name is (Michael). It's a pleasure (knowing) you.

저는 (텍사스)에 살아요. 이곳은 (도시)에요. 제 별명은 (피카츄)에요.
I live in Texas. It is a city. My nickname is Pikachu.

저는 (앰버 씨)에게 편지 쓰려고 한국어를 공부해요.
I study Korean so I can write a letter to (앰버 씨=you).

한국에 가보고 싶어요. 항상 보고싶어요.
I want to visit Korea. I always mis you.

당신과 같은 사람은 이 세상에 없어요. 덕분에 매일 행복해요.
There is no one like you in the world. Thanks to you, I am happy everyday.

고마움에 보답할게요.
I will repay you for your kindness.

시간 내서 편지 읽어줘서 고마워요.
Thank you for taking the time to read my letter.

잘 지내요!
Take care!

(마이클)이
From (Michael)

(효린 누나)에게
Dear (Hyorin nuna),

해냈어요! 대상 타신것 축하해요! 그럴 자격이
있어요.You did it! Congratulations on winning
the daesang (grand prize)! You deserve it.

새 앨범에 있는 곡들 전부 다 좋아요. 최고중의
최고에요. 제 느낌은 틀린적이 없어요.
I like every single song in the album. You are
the best of the best. My feelings have never
been wrong.

너무 열심히 일하지 마세요. 파티 너무 많이 하
지 마세요. 음주운전은 절대 안되요!
Don't work too hard. Don't party too hard.
Drunk driving is never okay!

자주 앨범 내 주세요.
Please release albums more often.

또 편지 할게요.
I will write you again.

(타일러)가
From (Tyler)

(슈가 오빠)에게
Dear (Suga oppa),

그동안 별 일 없었어요? 정말 오랜만이에요!
It really has been a long time! Anything new down your way?

(콘서트)**에서 (오빠)* 를 보았어요.
I saw (you)* at/in the (concert)**.

(오빠) 가 나와 같은 하늘 아래에 살고 있다는 사실에 기분이 너무좋아요.
The fact that (oppa=you) and I live under the same sky (in the same world) makes me feel so happy.

고맙다는 표현을 어떻게 해야 충분한지 모르겠어요. 부끄러움을 좀 타지만, 고마워요.
I don't know how to thank you enough. I am a little shy to say this, but thank you.

이 세상에 단 하나뿐인 존재가 되어줘서 고마워요.
Thank you for being the one and only.

군대에서 돌아올때까지 기다릴게요.

I will wait until you come back from the army.

(해나)가
From (Hannah)

사랑하는 (이특 오빠)에게
To my dearest (Lee Teuk oppa),

생일 축하합니다!
Happy Birthday!

(오빠) 는 하늘이 주신 선물이에요. (오빠)는 세상에 단 하나밖에 없는 사람이에요.
(Oppa=you) are a gift from heaven. You are the one and only person in the world.

술 너무 많이 마시지 마세요. 몸에 좋은 것 많이 먹어요.
Don't drink too much. Eat lots of things that are good for your body.

(오빠) 행복이 (저)의 행복이에요! (오빠) 가 항상 제 곁에 있어주었으면 좋겠어요.
(Your) happiness is (my) happiness! I always want to have (you) right here by my side.

팬들을 위해 열심히 해주세요!
Please do your very best for the fans!

제 선물 마음에 들었으면 좋겠어요!
I hope you like my gift!

선물을 보면 제 생각을 해 주세요.
Please think of me when you look at my gift.

행운의 여신이 함께 하기를!
May the lady luck be with you!

시간 내서 편지 읽어줘서 고마워요.
Thank you for taking the time to read my
letter.

행복하세요!
Be happy!

(신디아) 가
From (Cynthia)

사랑하는 (현아 누나)에게
To my dearest (Hyuna noona),

잘 지냈어요? 오랜만에 편지를 써요.
How have you been? It's been a while since I
wrote to you.

(사인회)** 에서 (누나)* 를 보았어요. 모두에게
친절해서 좋아요.
I saw (nuna=you)* at the (fan signing)**. I
like the fact that you are kind to everyone.

몸매가 정말 좋으세요. 어떻게 몸매를 유지해
요? 정말 완벽해요. 언제부터 그렇게 (예뻤어
요)?
You are in such great shape. How do you
stay in shape? You are really perfect. Since
when have you been so (pretty)?

모든걸 다 가진 사람이에요. 훌륭한 아내가 될
거에요.
You are a man who has everything. You will
make a great wife.

(누나) 를 사랑하는 팬들이 정말 많아요.
There are many fans who love (you).

(우리)가 (콘서트)에 응원하러 갈거에요.
We will be at the (concert) to support you.

큰 소리로 외칠거에요.I will cry at the top of
my voice.

함께 노래 할거에요. 형광봉을 흔들거에요.
I will sing along with you. I will be waving a
light stick.

팬들을 위해 열심히 해주세요!
Please do your very best for the fans!

신의 가호가 있기를!
May the grace of God be with you!

잘 지내요!
Take care!

(카를로스)가
From Carlos

~ Useful Conjunction / Transition Words ~

그리고 – And 그러나 – But 하지만 – However

무엇보다 – Above all 그래도 – Nevertheless

아참! – Oh! (When something suddenly comes to your mind)

그래서 – As a result 물론 – Of course

아쉽게도 – Regrettably 사실 – In fact

그렇기는 하지만 – Even so

우습게도 – Funny enough

제 생각에는 – In my opinion

특이하게도 – Strangely enough

믿기 어렵지만 – Although it's hard to believe

불행하게도 – Unfortunately

How to Write
Common
Names in
Hangul
Korean Alphabet

Abel – 아벨
Abigail – 아비가일
Abraham – 에이브러햄
Ace – 에이스
Ada – 아다
Adam – 아담
Adela – 아델
Adelio – 아델리오
Adolph – 아돌프
Adonis – 아도니스
Adora – 아도라
Agatha – 아가타
Aggie – 애기
Agnes – 아그네스
Aida – 아이다
Aileen – 에일린
Ailish – 앨리쉬
Aimee – 에이미
Alan, Allan – 앨런
Albert – 앨버트
Albino – 앨비노
Alex – 알렉스
Alexa – 알렉사
Alexis – 알렉시스
Alexandra – 알렉산드라
Alexandria – 알렉산드리아
Alexander – 알렉산더
Alfred – 알프레드
Ali – 알리
Alice – 앨리스
Alicia – 앨리샤
Alika – 앨리카
Allie – 앨리
Allison – 앨리슨
Aloha – 알로하
Alvin – 앨빈
Alyssa – 앨리사
Amanda – 아만다
Amber – 앰버
Ami – 아미

Amos – 아모스
Amy – 에이미
Anais – 아나이스
Andra – 안드라
Andrea – 안드레아
Andrew – 앤드류
Andy – 앤디
Angel – 엔젤
Angela – 앤젤러
Angelica – 안젤리카
Anika – 애니카
Anna – 안나
Annie – 애니
Anthony – 안토니
Apollo – 아폴로
Aria – 아리아
Ariel – 아리엘
Arista – 아리스타
Arnold – 아놀드
Aaron – 아론
Arthur – 아서
Arvid – 아비드
Asha – 아샤
Ashley – 애슐리
Aster – 아스터
Astin – 아스틴
Aurora – 오로라
Austin – 오스틴
Autumn – 오텀
Ava – 아바
Baba – 바바
Bailey – 베일리
Bambi – 밤비
Barbara – 바바라
Barbie – 바비
Barley – 발리
Barney – 바니
Baron – 바론
Basil – 배즐
Baxter – 백스터

Beatrice - 비아트리스
Beau - 보우
Bebe - 베베
Beck - 벡
Becky - 베키
Belita - 벨리타
Bella - 벨라
Belle - 벨
Benecia - 베네치아
Benedict - 베네딕트
Benny - 베니
Benjamin - 벤자민
Berg - 버그
Bessie - 베시
Biana - 비안나
Bianca - 비앙카
Bibiane - 비비안
Billy - 빌리
Bingo - 빙고
Bishop - 비숍
Bliss - 블리스
Blondie - 블론디
Bonita - 보니타
Bono - 보노
Boris - 보리스
Boss - 보스
Brainna - 브래나
Brandon - 브랜든
Breanna - 브리나
Brian - 브라이언
Briana - 브리아나
Bridget - 브리지트
Bright - 브라이트
Brittany - 브리태니
Brooke - 브루크
Bruno - 브루노
Buck - 벅
Buddy - 버디
Bunny - 버니
Caesar - 시저

Caleb - 케일럽
Caley - 캘리
Calix - 캘릭스
Calla - 칼라
Callia - 칼리아
Cameron - 카메론
Camilla - 카밀라
Captain - 캡틴
Cara - 카라
Carmel - 카멜
Carmen - 카르멘
Caroline - 캐롤라인
Carlos - 카를로스
Cassandra - 카산드라
Casey - 캐시
Cassidy - 캐시디
Catherine - 캐서린
Cecil - 세실
Celestyn - 셀레스틴
Celina - 셀리나
Cha Cha - 샤샤
Chloe - 클로에
Champ - 챔프
Charles - 찰스
Charlie - 찰리
Chase - 체이스
Chavi - 샤비
Chelsea - 첼시
Cherie - 쉐리
Chloe - 클로에
Chrissy - 크리시
Christian - 크리스챤
Christina - 크리스티나
Christopher - 크리스토퍼
Cindy - 신디
Clara - 클라라
Clark - 클락
Claude - 클라우드
Claudia - 클라우디아
Cleo - 클레오

Cleta – 클레타
Coco – 코코
Cody – 코디
Colin – 콜린
Connie – 코니
Conrad – 콘라드
Corby – 코비
Crystal – 크리스탈
Courtney – 코트니
Cyclone – 사이클론
Cyma – 시마
Daina – 데이나
Daisy – 데이지
Dali – 달리
Daniel – 다니엘
Danielle – 다니엘레
Danika – 다니카
Darby – 다비
Daria – 다리아
Darin – 다린
Dario – 다리오
Darwin – 다윈
Dave – 데이브
David – 다비드
Dean – 딘
Della – 델라
Delling – 델링
Delphine – 델핀
Dennis – 데니스
Derry – 데리
Destiny – 데스티니
Deva – 데바
Dexter – 덱스터
Diallo – 디알로
Dick – 딕
Dino – 디노
Dixie – 딕시
Donald – 도널드
Donna – 돈나
Doris – 도리스

Dorothy – 도로시
Douglas – 더글라스
Duke – 듀크
Duncan – 던컨
Dustin – 더스틴
Dylan, Dillon – 딜런
Dyllis – 딜리스
Eavan – 에반
Ebony – 에보니
Edan – 에단
Edeline – 에델린
Eden – 에덴
Edgar – 에드가
Edith – 에디스
Edmund – 에드문드
Edward – 에드워드
Edwin – 에드윈
Eilis – 엘리스
Eldora – 엘도라
Elin – 엘린
Elisha – 엘리샤
Elizabeth – 엘리자베스
Elle – 엘르
Elroy – 엘로이
Elsa – 엘사
Elvis – 엘비스
Elysia – 엘리시아
Emilie, Emily – 에밀리
Emery – 에머리
Emma – 엠마
Enoch – 에녹
Eric – 에릭
Erica – 에리카
Erin – 에린
Eris – 에리스
Esteban – 에스테반
Esther – 에스더
Ethan – 에단
Eugene – 유진
Eva – 에바

Evan – 에반	Harold – 해럴드
Eve – 이브	Harry – 해리
Evelyn – 이벨린	Heba – 헤바
Farrell – 파렐	Helen – 헬렌
Favian – 파비앙	Helia – 헬리아
Fedora – 페도라	Henry – 헨리
Ferdianand – 퍼디난드	Hera – 헤라
Felice – 펠리체	Hubert – 휴버트
Felix – 펠릭스	Huey – 휴이
Fella – 펠라	Hugh – 휴
Fidelio – 피델리오	Humphery – 험프리
Filia – 필리아	Hunter – 헌터
Fleta – 플레타	Ian – 이안
Florence – 플로렌스	Iliana – 일리아나
Floria – 플로리아	Indira – 인디라
Forrest – 포레스트	Ingrid – 잉그리드
Frederick – 프레데릭	Irene – 아이린
Freeman – 프리맨	Irina – 아이리나
Frances – 프란시스	Iris – 아이리스
Gabriel – 가브리엘	Isaac, Issac – 아이작
Gabriella – 가브리엘라	Isabel – 이사벨
Gemma – 젬마	Isadora – 이사도라
Geoffrey – 제프리	Jace – 제이스
George – 조지	Jack – 잭
Gilbert – 길버트	Jackson – 잭슨
Gili – 길리	Jacob – 제이콥
Giovanni – 지오반니	Jaclyn – 재클린
Gloria – 글로리아	Jade – 제이드
Goofy – 구피	James – 제임스
Grace – 그레이스	Jane – 제인
Grania – 그라니아	Jasmine – 쟈스민
Gregory – 그레고리	Jason – 제이슨
Hailey – 헤일리	Jasper – 제스퍼
Haley – 할리	Jefferson – 제퍼슨
Halona – 할로나	Jeffrey – 제프리
Hannah – 한나	Jenna – 제나
Happy – 해피	Jennifer – 제니퍼
Harace – 헤레이스	Jennie– 제니
Harley – 할리	Jeremy – 제레미
	Jericho – 제리코

Jerome – 제롬
Jerry – 제리
Jess – 제스
Jessica – 제시카
Jessie – 제시
Jesus – 헤수스 (Spanish)
Jodie – 조디
Johanna – 조안나
John – 존
Jolly – 졸리
Jonathan – 조나단
Jordan – 조단
Joseph – 조셉
Joshua – 죠수아
Joy – 조이
Jud – 쥬드
Judith – 쥬디스
Julia – 쥴리아
Juliana – 쥴리아나
Juliet – 쥴리엣
Justin – 져스틴
Kali – 칼리
Kara – 카라
Karena – 카레나
Karis – 카리스
Kassia – 카시아
Kate – 케이트
Katherine, Kathryn – 케서린
Kathy – 케티
Katie – 케이티
Kaitlyn – 케이슬린
Kayla – 카일라
Kaylee – 카일리
Kellan – 켈란
Kelley – 켈리
Kelsey – 켈시
Kenneth – 케네스
Kerri – 케리
Kevin – 케빈
Kiara – 키아라

Kimberly – 킴벌리
Klaus – 클라우스
Kori – 코리
Kuper – 쿠퍼
Kyle – 카일
Kylie – 카일
Kyra – 키라
Lakia – 라키아
Lala – 랄라
Lamis – 라미스
Lani – 라니
Lappy – 래피
Lara – 라라
Laura – 로라
Lauren – 로렌
Lavina – 라비나
Lawrence – 로렌스
Lee – 리
Leena – 리나
Lelia – 렐리아
Leo – 레오
Leonard – 레오나드
Leopold – 레오폴드
Leslie – 레슬리
Lev – 레브
Lewis, Louis, Luis – 루이스
Lidia – 리디아
Lily – 릴리
Lina – 리나
Linda – 린다
Lisa – 리사
Lloyd – 로이드
Lonnie – 로니
Lottie – 로티
Louis – 루이스
Lowell – 로웰
Lucia – 루시아
Lucifer – 루시퍼
Lucy – 루시

Lukas – 루카스
Luna – 루나
Mabel – 마벨
Mackenzie – 맥킨지
Madeline – 마들린
Madison – 메디슨
Madonna – 마돈나
Maggie – 매기
Makaio – 마카이오
Makayla – 마케이라
Malissa – 맬리사
Malo – 말로
Mana – 마나
Mandelina – 만델리나
Manon – 마농
Marcia – 마르샤
Margaret – 마가레트
Maria – 마리아
Mariah – 마리아
Marissa – 마리사
Martha – 마사
Martin – 마틴
Mary – 매리
Mathilda – 마틸다
Matthew – 매튜
Maya – 마야
Megan – 메건
Melina – 멜리나
Melissa – 멜리사
Meriel – 메리엘
Michael – 마이클
Michelle – 미쉘
Mickey – 미키
Minnie – 미니
Miranda – 미란다
Misty – 미스티
Molly – 몰리
Monet – 모네
Monica – 모니카
Morgan – 모건

Morris – 모리스
Murphy – 머피
Nadia – 나디아
Nami – 나미
Nana – 나나
Nani – 나니
Naomi – 나오미
Nara – 나라
Narcisse – 나르시스
Natalie – 나탈리
Nathan – 네이탄
Navid – 나비드
Neal – 닐
Neema – 니마
Nero – 네로
Nia – 니아
Nicholas – 니콜라스
Nicole – 니콜
Nicky – 닉키
Nina – 니나
Noah – 노아
Noel – 노엘
Odelia – 오델리아
Olga – 올가
Olive – 올리브
Oliver – 올리버
Olivia – 올리비아
Oscar – 오스카
Owen – 오웬
Pablo – 파블로
Paige – 페이지
Paloma – 팔로마
Pamela – 파멜라
Patricia – 패트리샤
Patrick – 패트릭
Paul – 폴
Pavel – 파벨
Peggy – 페기
Pello – 펠로
Penda – 펜다

Peppi – 페피
Peter – 피터
Petra – 페트라
Phila – 필라
Phillip – 필립
Phyllis – 필리스
Pinky – 핑키
Pluto – 플루토
Poco – 포코
Polo – 폴로
Pooky – 푸키
Poppy – 포피
Primo – 프리모
Prince – 프린스
Princess – 프린세스
Puffy – 퍼피
Rachel – 레이첼
Rabia – 라비아
Raina – 레이나
Ralph – 랄프
Rania – 라니아
Ravi – 라비
Rebecca – 레베카
Redford – 레드포드
Reggie – 레지
Rei – 레이
Remy – 레미
Rex – 렉스
Richard – 리차드
Ricky – 리키
Riley – 라일리
Ringo – 링고
Rio – 리오
Risa – 리사
Robbie – 로비
Robert – 로버트
Robin – 로빈
Rocky – 록키
Roja – 로하
Roland – 롤랜드
Rollo – 롤로
Romeo – 로미오

Roland – 롤랜드
Rollo – 롤로
Romeo – 로미오
Rosemary – 로즈마리
Rosie – 로지
Roxy – 록시
Roy – 로이
Ruby – 루비
Rudolph – 루돌프
Rudy – 루디
Ryan – 라이언
Sebastian – 세바스찬
Sabrina – 사브리나
Sally – 샐리
Salvatore – 살바토레
Sam – 샘
Samantha – 사만다
Samson – 샘슨
Samuel – 새뮤엘
Sandy – 샌디
Sarah – 사라
Sasha – 사샤
Savannah – 사바나
Scarlet – 스칼렛
Scoop – 스쿠프
Sebastian – 세바스찬
Selina – 셀리나
Selma – 셀마
Serena – 세레나
Shaina – 샤이나
Shasa – 샤사
Shelby – 셸비
Sheri – 쉐리
Sierra – 시에라
Silvester – 실베스터
Simon – 사이먼
Solomon – 솔로몬
Sonia – 쏘냐
Sonny – 써니
Sophia, Sophie – 소피아, 소피

Sunny — 써니
Syndey — 시드니
Sylvester — 실베스터
Sylvia — 실비아
Talia — 탈리아
Talli — 탈리
Tanesia — 타네시아
Tania — 타냐
Taylor, Tailor — 테일러
Ted — 테드
Tess — 테스
Theodore — 시오도어
Thomas — 토머스
Timothy — 티모시
Tomo — 토모
Trisha — 트리샤
Tyler — 타일러
Umberto — 움베르토
Valencia — 발렌시아
Vanessa — 바네사
Vera — 베라
Verdi — 베르디
Veronica — 베로니카
Victoria — 빅토리아
Vincent — 빈센트
Violet — 바이올렛
Vivian — 비비안
Waldo — 왈도
Walter — 월터
Wallace — 월러스
Wendy — 웬디
William — 윌리엄
Wily — 윌리
Winston — 윈스톤
Woody — 우디
Yuki — 유키
Zachary — 재커리
Zena — 제나
Zenia — 제니아
Zeppelin — 제플린

If your name is not listed, try

http://roman.cs.pusan.ac.kr

You can type your English name and it will convert it into Korean Hangul.

Made in the USA
San Bernardino, CA
18 December 2017